The
Quaker
Parrot

An Owner's Guide To

A HAPPY HEALTHY PET

Howell Book House

Howell Book House
A Simon & Schuster Macmillan Company
1633 Broadway
New York, NY 10019

Macmillan Publishing books may be purchased for business or sales promotional use. For information please write: Special Markets Department, Macmillan Publishing USA, 1633 Broadway, New York, NY 10019.

Library of Congress Cataloging-in-Publication Data
Higdon, Pamela Leis.
The quaker parrot: an owner's guide to a happy, healthy pet
  / Pamela Leis Higdon.
p. cm.
ISBN: 0-87605448-3
1. Quaker Parrots. I. Title. II. Series.
SF473.M65H54   1998
636.6'865—dc21   97-41806
               CIP

Manufactured in the United States of America
10 9 8 7 6 5 4 3 2 1

Series Director: Amanda Pisani
Series Assistant Director: Jennifer Liberts
Book Design by Michele Laseau
Cover Design by Iris Jeromnimon
Illustration by Laura Robbins
Photography:
  Front cover by Eric Ilasenko
  Back cover by Renée Stockdale
  Kelli Cates: 81, 93
  Sherry Lee Harris: 14
  Eric Ilasenko: i, 2-3, 5, 10, 17, 18, 21, 30, 38, 40, 42, 43, 44, 52, 58, 61, 62, 74, 91, 94, 100, 113, 115, 121
  David Schilling: 12, 27, 46, 107
  D. Shulman, courtesy of 33rd and Bird: 9, 23, 29, 110
  Renée Stockdale: 6, 8, 11, 13, 15, 19, 20, 22, 24, 25, 33, 34, 36-37, 39, 41, 45, 48, 49, 50, 54, 55, 56, 59, 65, 67, 69, 71, 73, 77, 78, 79, 80, 82, 83, 84, 86, 87, 88, 89, 95, 96, 97, 101, 102, 104, 108-109, 112, 114, 115, 116, 117, 118, 119, 122
Production Team: Toi Davis, Natalie Hollifield, Stephanie Hammett, Clint Lahnen, Stephanie Mohler, Dennis Sheehan, Terri Sheehan

Contents

Welcome
to the
World

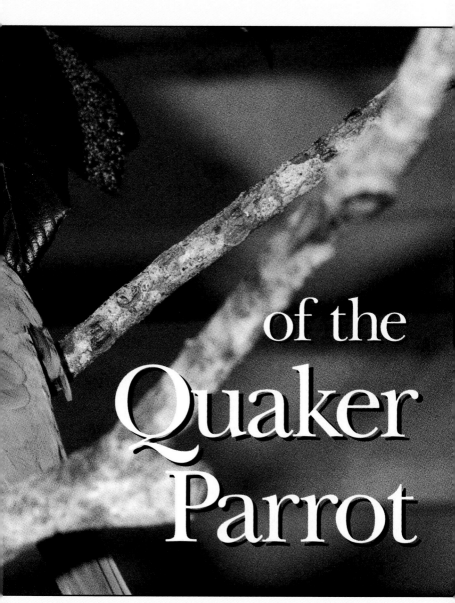

of the
Quaker Parrot

External Features of the Quaker Parrot

Crown

Nares

Eye

Cere

Nape

Mantle

Beak

Breast

Wing

Claw

Tail Feathers

What Is a Parrot?

Whether you have bought this book and are now sitting down to read it, or you are leafing through it considering its purchase, you are probably interested in birds. I have been fascinated with birds from childhood. Our interest makes us want to buy them and bring them home to share our lives. Sometimes we fall in love with the stories we read in books, magazines or on the Internet. Sometimes the lure of birds is generated by those we see on television, both real and computer animated. However birds came to your attention, you owe it to yourself, to your family and,

most of all, to the bird you are considering to learn as much as you can about its species and about the individual bird before you bring her home.

5

Characteristics of Birds

I have noticed, as I'm sure you have, too, that each bird species not only looks different from other birds, but also has special personality characteristics common to most of its members. Among wild birds, for instance, the various kinds of blue jays are bold and raucous; doves, on the other hand, are often timid, flying away at the slightest hint of danger. Some birds, like crows or grackles, are noisy. Others, like kinglets, chickadees or cardinals, are quiet, making only small, pleasant sounds.

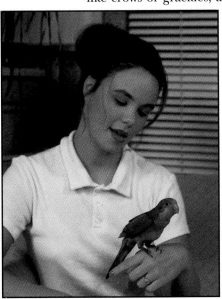

All pet bird species are wild birds somewhere on this earth, and members of their species share certain general characteristics. For this reason, I stress to anyone considering a bird that the most important thing you can do before buying one is to make sure that the bird's personality and needs mesh with your own.

Before you purchase a Quaker parrot, make sure her personality characteristics are compatible with your lifestyle.

While it is true that birds do not require a daily walk, a great deal of space or a litter box, they do require love and companionship, understanding, a balanced diet and knowledgeable care. A treasured, properly cared for, healthy Quaker parrot may live as long as thirty-five to forty years. One that is poorly cared for will live less than five years.

If you have considered carefully and have chosen the right bird for your personality and lifestyle, every year with your Quaker can be a delight. You will always know what to expect and how to keep your bird happy and healthy. Her species characteristics, such as her energy level and need for companionship, will match your personality. If you've made an educated choice, your budget can easily include the needs of your bird, and your family agrees with the addition of this feathered member and has learned how to handle her.

Is a Quaker parrot really the best bird for you? The information in this book should help you decide. As you read, consider whether the needs of this active, intelligent imp of a parrot will fit your personality and lifestyle. A close match will help to ensure that you and a Quaker parrot will make great, lifelong companions.

Early Birds: Which Came First?

The first birds lived on earth long before humans, in the days of the dinosaur during the Jurassic Period. Occupying the air with the first birds were flying reptiles, which had begun to develop about thirty-five million years before those early birds. At this time, we believe that *Archeopteryx lithographica* was the first feathered, flying animal, or bird. We continue to hope that later discoveries in Texas and other places around the world will turn up other links in avian history.

By studying fossils, paleontologists have learned that the first birds lived about 140 million years ago in cycad forests, and were about the size of a present-day crow. Cycads are tropical and semi-tropical cone-bearing plants similar to palm trees.

Experts disagree on when parrots developed. Some accept *Archeopteryx verreauxi*, found in France and dating from about thirty million years ago, as the first parrot. Others believe *Conuropsis fratercula*, found in Nebraska and dating from twenty million years ago, is the most parrot-like of ancient birds. Fossils of other parrots found in South America date from at least one million years ago.

> ### DID YOU KNOW?
>
> The largest parrot in the world is the Hyacinth Macaw (about 3 feet long) from South America. The smallest is the 3-inch-long Pygmy parrot from New Guinea. South America and Australia have many native parrot species; Africa has only a few. North America had two native species, the Carolina parakeet and the Thick-billed parrot. Accounts from the 1800s report clouds of these birds. Hunters killed both types of parrots to extinction in the United States.
>
> Populations of Thick-billed parrots still live wild in Mexico and in captivity in the United States—an exceptionally strong population resides in the Sacramento Zoo in California. Presently, attempts to re-introduce Thick-billed parrots into the southwestern United States have been largely unsuccessful.

Today, more than 8,000 species of birds live all over the earth. Their numbers are in constant decline, however, because of the loss of habitat and the vast numbers of wild birds captured for sale as pets. Of those that remain today, about 350 species are parrots.

Parrot Characteristics

Parrots come in many shapes and sizes. The most distinctive feature they all have is their beak. The curved upper mandible that fits neatly into the lower mandible works well to break open seeds, nuts, bones and other foods relished by parrots. The tongue is thick and strong; it is used with the beak to remove foods from husks, shells or other coverings.

Parrots have broad skulls and short, skinny necks. The first time you feel a parrot neck, you may be in for a surprise. It feels like a chicken or turkey neck—thin and bony. This neck is surprisingly mobile. A parrot can move her head 180° very quickly. Like other birds, parrots have excellent eyesight, far better than that of any human.

All parrots have beaks that are distinguished by a curved upper mandible that fits neatly into the lower mandible.

Parrots have distinctive feet, shared by only a few other birds, including woodpeckers. Two toes point forward and two point backward. This arrangement allows them to grip branches and other perches, as well as to walk with a waddling gait on the ground. Some parrots use their feet to grasp food as they eat. Some may stand on larger pieces of food to secure them as they eat. Still others seem not to have learned to stabilize food in any way, eating it only if it is secured to a branch or is resting on a flat surface.

FACTS ABOUT FEATHERS

Feathers cover all parts of a parrot—from her head to the tip of her tail. Only her beak, eyes, eye lids, legs, feet and toenails remain uncovered by feathers. The layer of feathers closest to the skin is called **down**. It is soft and fluffy and helps keep the bird warm. Parrots also have **powder barbs**, which are a kind of down feather. These feathers grow throughout a parrot's life and break off into bits so fine they resemble dust or powder. Some species have more powder down feathers than others; cockatoos, for instance, are noted for their heavy powder. This powder helps keep parrot feathers clean.

The outer feathers are called **contour feathers** and include those on the wings and tail. These are the feathers you will see first; they cover the outline, or contour, of the bird and come in various colors. Current thinking on the matter is that colors serve as either good camouflage in the bird's native habitat or as a way to attract a mate.

Parrots have unique feet, with two toes that point forward and two that point backward.

chapter 2

All **About**
Quaker Parrots

A Quaker parrot is a medium-size bird, about 11 to 13 inches (29 cm) long from his head to the tip of his long, tapered tail—approximately the size of a cockatiel. The Quaker has a heftier build and body than a cockatiel, however.

Quaker Colors

The basic, or ground, colors of this bird are green and gray. Adults of the nominate race, *Myiopsitta monachus*, have a blue-gray forehead. The lores, cheeks and throat are pale gray. Feathers on the throat and abdomen are edged in a lighter gray, giving them a scalloped, or barred, look. Feathers below these on the abdomen are olive green, becoming a yellowish green on the lower abdomen, legs and under the tail. The nape of the neck is bright green, and the mantle and wings are a dull green. The lower back and rump are a brighter yellow green, as are the underwing coverts and undersides of the flight feathers.

Quaker parrots are about 11 to 13 inches (29 cm) long.

Making a beautiful contrast with the gray and green feathers, the primary coverts, outer primaries and secondary feathers are blue. Some green tail feathers are further accented by the lovely blue of the down feathers in that area. The beak is a light pinkish-brown color, and the legs are gray. The eyes are brown. Males and females are not sexually dimorphic: They have the same outward appearance—to everyone but other Quaker parrots.

ARE QUAKERS MONKS?

In many countries other than the United States, Quakers are known as Monk parakeets, probably because their coloring—particularly the contrast between green and gray—looks similar to a monk's cloak and hood. The origin of the name Quaker parakeet is unknown, although several theories abound. The Duke of Bedford, a well-known aviculturist who died unexpectedly in 1953, talked about Quakers in a book published in 1969. He wrote, "The Quaker is a noisy bird, continually uttering its 'Quak, quaki, quakwi, quak-wi, quarr! quarr! quarr!'" Perhaps this is

11

where the name came from. On the other hand, Michele Lowell wrote in *Your Pet Bird, A Buyer's Guide*, "This greenish parrot (*Myiopsitta monachus*), also called monk parakeet, is named for his unusual gray bib, reminiscent of the old-fashioned Quaker costume pictured on the Quaker Oats box." Mattie Sue Athan, a noted avian behaviorist and author, believes the name is derived from the way chicks' bodies shake when they beg for food.

Quakers are also known as Monk parakeets—possibly because their coloring looks like a monk's cloak and hood.

Classification of Quaker Parrots

Quaker parrots are also called Gray-breasted parakeets and sometimes Gray-headed parakeets. Scientific classification of birds (and other species) is important even to those of us who are simply interested in a bird as a pet. Use of the scientific name helps to avoid the problems that could arise from the use of common names: Birds and other animals are known by many names in different countries, or in different parts of countries. By using the scientific name, we can be sure we are talking about the same bird or other form of life.

Scientific classification depends on several factors. Elements taken into account include feeding habits, reproductive habits, anatomy and physiology, as well as DNA. Birds comprise a large and varied group of animals. They are then divided into more specific groups. Quaker parrots have small bodies with long, slender, graduated tails, which makes them seem close anatomically to conures and parakeets. When other factors are taken into account, however, they seem to have more in common with parakeets than with conures.

Quakers are classified as belonging to the order *Psitta-ciformes*. They are members of the genus *Myiopsitta*. There are four subspecies: *Myiopsitta monachus (M.m.) monachus, Monacus, M.m. calita, M.m. cotorra* and *M.m. luchsi*. These are New World parrots from South America.

Quaker Parrots in the Wild

In the wild, Quaker parrots are usually found near large water sources, such as lakes and rivers, in lowland areas of Paraguay, Bolivia, Argentina and Brazil. They inhabit open savannas, scrub forests and palm groves, especially where rainfall is low. They are bold birds and can also be found in South American city parks, on farms and in yards.

Here are a pair of M.m. mona-chus, otherwise known as Quaker parrots.

Quaker parrots are fascinating for many reasons, but their nesting habits are unique among parrots; they build their own nests, while other parrots use existing sites, such as tree cavities, as the basis for their nests. Quakers weave sticks, twigs, small branches and other materials into complex structures. Groups of wild Quakers live together, each pair with its own residence comprising at least two chambers. Each compartment serves a different purpose, including one for egg incubation or a place to feed young chicks, another in which to feed older chicks and a third from which parents can keep a watch for danger.

As the flock grows, each pair builds its apartment onto the main nest, resulting in some huge nests after many years. Quakers also tolerate the presence of other bird species that seem not to threaten Quakers, such as ducks. Some reports have older Quaker colony nests

13

weighing half a ton, or a thousand pounds. A nest that had become quite famous in Bridgeport, Connecticut, was knocked down in a storm several years ago. It reportedly weighed about 50 pounds. Local residents took in chicks that survived the storm.

THE ADAPTABLE QUAKER

Wild Quakers do not shy away from humans and can be found in and near both small and large towns, as well as farms and orchards. This fearlessness, coupled with the Quaker's willingness to raid cultivated crops

for food, has led to large-scale hunting and attempts to eradicate the bird in his native habitat, where many consider Quakers agricultural pests.

Wild Quaker parrots are highly adaptable; they have readily taken up residence in eucalyptus trees, which were introduced to South America from Australia many years ago. Wild feral colonies of Quaker parrots can also be found in Puerto Rico and several parts of

Unlike other parrots who inhabit existing sites, Quaker parrots build their own nests out of twigs and small branches.

the United States, including California, Colorado, Connecticut, Florida, Hawaii, Illinois, Massachusetts, New Jersey, New York, North Carolina, Ohio, Oklahoma, Texas and Virginia. Cold weather and snow common to some of those locations do not seem to deter the hardy Quaker from not only surviving, but thriving.

Color Mutations

The word "mutation" appears in several sections of this book. A mutation is a change in a normal characteristic, such as color, that can occur spontaneously for no apparent reason. In the wild, a bird (or other animal) with a color mutation probably will not survive. Others of its species may not recognize it as one of their own and may kill it. This instinctive reaction to a bird that is different from the group may help to ensure the survival of the rest of the species in the wild.

In captivity, however, many mutations are prized. Breeders mate birds that show prized mutated characteristics or that may have hidden potential for such characteristics because of their inherited genetics. Unusual color mutations in pet birds are highly valued and breeders work hard to achieve them. In this way, breeders have developed some beautiful Quaker parrot colors not seen in the wild, such as blue, yellow, cinnamon, pied (a combination of green and yellow in a varied pattern), albinos and, some indicate, a yellow-faced Quaker parakeet. Such mutations are prized by many collectors, making them much more expensive than normal Quakers. The more difficult it is to find, the more expensive the mutation will be.

The Quaker's tail feathers are green, with dark blue in the center of each, when viewed from above.

A bird with a rare mutation will not make a better pet than standard Quaker parrots, which can be found all over the country at reasonable prices. The availability of standard birds also means that you are more likely to find a healthy, tamed, wonderful pet bird among them than you might among the smaller numbers of rare mutations.

The Quaker Parrot's Arrival
It is difficult to pinpoint the date of the arrival of the first Quaker parrot in Europe or the United States. We do know, however, that they were firmly established in Europe by the 1950s. The Duke of Bedford, who wrote a book on parrots at that time, told of Quakers in Germany; one in particular was an amusing talker

and did tricks on command. Quakers must surely have been well established in the United States, too, by then.

In a time when air travel was reserved for those in the military or those with enough money to travel on commercial or private carriers, it would have been far easier to ship Quaker parrots to North America than to Europe. By the 1960s, enough Quaker parrots had escaped confinement in the United States to form the first feral colonies. Many sources believe that a consignment of Quakers shipped by air to New York in the '60s escaped and formed colonies in New York City. Other escapees became legendary during the next twenty years in such widely separated states as Connecticut, New Jersey, Illinois, Florida and Texas.

A QUESTION OF LEGALITY

According to a representative from the California Department of Agriculture, Quakers are considered a pest bird species, based on reports from governments of South American countries where the birds originate. Quakers are illegal in California under any circumstances, despite the lack of any documented evidence of crop destruction in the state by feral (wild) colonies of Quakers.

Embassies, consulates and United Nations representatives of countries such as Argentina (where the birds are native) claim that the birds are pest species in their habitat, destroying as much as two-thirds of the grain crops planted each year. Even if you accept that figure, and I find it difficult to believe, why is this bird considered more of a problem than, for example,

---

CITY BIRDS?

While I was doing research on Quakers for *Bird Talk* magazine, a reader called to tell me that one large nest in Hyde Park, Chicago, Illinois, had been threatened by local residents who disliked the noise the birds tend to generate in large flocks. When I called to check out the story, I found that the nest was protected—by a high-ranking member of the police force who lived nearby.

Quakers thrive in many Texas cities, no matter how severe the winters become. In Houston, for example, the birds often make nests on electric towers. Light and power workers take down nests and sell the chicks at reasonable prices to prevent people from climbing the towers and endangering themselves and others in a foolish attempt to get a free parrot. The potential for damage to power lines and transformers is also avoided by this removal.

cockatoos? Cockatoos are considered a pest species in Australia, their native habitat, but are legal in all parts of North America.

Due to their great adaptability, Quaker parrots have been able to thrive in severe climates and terrain.

Parrots all over the world have similar habits: They descend in a large, noisy group, and they eat and destroy, leaving farmers with ruined crops. From an economic point of view, the attack by a group of parrots would be devastating to any farmer or rancher. But why have agricultural interests in some American states singled out Quakers for punitive legislation?

Quakers are different from most parrots in that they have a remarkable ability to survive even cold, wet temperatures. Add this to the fact that they breed easily and tend to live in large flocks, and you soon have some American agricultural interests panicked. This hysteria, brought to some state legislators, resulted in the passage of laws outlawing the birds under any circumstances.

THE PARROT'S PLACE IN HISTORY

Paintings and literature reveal that parrots were kept in captivity in Asian, Middle Eastern and European cultures hundreds of years ago. It is believed by many that Alexander the Great may have been among the first to bring tame parrots to Europe from Asia. The Alexandrine parakeet (*Psittacula cyanocephala*) is named after this legendary warrior. Roman nobility kept parrots as a sign of status. Later, when European explorers began extending their searches for new and interesting treasures farther abroad, they sent home many parrots, especially during the 15th and 16th centuries.

The reaction is due, in part, to ignorance as well as fear. Most of the state laws in effect today stem from the 1970s and 1980s, before any serious studies on Quakers had begun in this country. Today, although some states remain steadfast in their anti-Quaker legislation, others are reconsidering.

Although some people interested in feral Quakers have reported that the birds rarely wander far from their nest site, I think this is true only if the birds have a reliable food source nearby. In South America, unless they live near urban or suburban areas where they can find food year-round, Quakers migrate in winter to find better food sources.

By the 1950s, Quaker parrots were well-established in the United States.

If I owned an orchard or grain crop within striking distance of a large flock of Quakers, I would admittedly be unhappy, but there are few enough flocks of wild Quakers that their locations are noted easily, and they do not appear to be spreading across the country at a rapid rate. This may be because most, if not all, feral Quakers in North America are located in or near cities, where food is available all year.

Argentine ornithologist Enrique E. Bucher believes Quakers fail to fit the typical profile of pest species because they (and other neotropical parrots) lack the "typical combination of high mobility, flock feeding and roosting, opportunistic breeding and high productivity that characterizes pest species."

Perhaps more encouraging from an agricultural point of view is the fact that wild-caught Quaker parrots are no longer imported into this country under an international agreement outlawing the importation of wild birds. While it is easy to see why a recently imported

Quaker could survive if he escaped, logic tells us that birds hand-fed, hand-raised and trained by humans would not survive easily in the wild. Even Quakers kept as pets for several years will surely lose the ability to survive on their own.

I believe that as time goes by, studies will prove that domestically bred Quakers are unlikely to have the ability to become feral pests. These studies, along with the increased recognition by Quaker owners that they must take steps to ensure their birds do not escape, may help some state agricultural representatives relax their restrictions.

Domestically bred Quakers are unlikely to have the ability to become feral pests.

As of publication, ownership of Quaker parrots is illegal in only seven states: California, Hawaii, Kentucky, Pennsylvania, Rhode Island, Tennessee and Wyoming. In Pennsylvania, any discovered Quaker parrot is euthanized. In addition, Kansas law makes it difficult to own a Quaker, requiring a permit that is difficult to obtain. Maine has made ownership legal, but it is also difficult to get the required permit. Georgia prohibits anyone from carrying Quakers across state lines, although it is not illegal to own one in that state. Ohio allows the birds to be kept if the wings are clipped. This state recently considered a more onerous law, outlawing all Quaker parrots, but public outcry seems to have delayed that attempt. Virginia makes ownership of them legal provided that the bird wears closed bands.

Keep in mind that laws change. If you are considering a Quaker, check with your state agricultural department before you buy a bird. The United States Agricultural Department does not keep records of individual state laws concerning birds.

Why Choose a Quaker Parrot?

Perhaps you have been thinking about buying a parrot—maybe you've even considered a Quaker parrot. What are the advantages of a Quaker parrot over other parrot species?

There are many. Quaker parrots are medium-size parrots, so they need only a relatively small cage compared to those needed to house larger parrots. Their manageable size means they are ideal both for apartments and homes. Quakers are hardy and suffer from few illnesses if kept clean and fed a balanced diet.

Quaker Parrot Particulars

If you appreciate energy, affection and intelligence in a pet and can delight in the humor of a Quaker's active, mischievous nature, a Quaker may be the perfect bird for you. If, on the other hand, you are too busy to give a bird a lot of attention, have valuable furniture or art objects or put a premium on neatness and want a pet that will always follow your rules, a Quaker is probably not a good bird for you.

MOST QUAKERS TALK

If a bird's potential for talking is an important factor in your choice, it's worth considering that many Quakers talk. Some owners report that they talk too well—repeating things said in moments of extreme pain or frustration and later regretted. Committed to a Quaker's memory after hearing it only once, such a word or phrase may be repeated often, at what the bird considers an appropriate time. It is almost impossible to erase a Quaker's memory of an emphatically stated word or phrase.

Many Quaker parrots talk, but even if yours doesn't, she'll still make a great pet.

Some Quakers learn to talk early and easily. Breeders have told me that their many handfed chicks begin talking before they are weaned. If you have your heart set on a bird that talks, ask the breeder or pet shop personnel to point out young birds that have already begun to talk.

Talking should never be the most important factor in your decision, however. It is the most unimportant aspect of a bird's personality. Treat it only like icing on the cake. If all other characteristics fit, then talking is the treat you can add to the package.

NEED A COMPANION?

Why do we want pets? We want them for the affection they provide and for the way they make us feel needed. Quakers are flock birds and they need companionship, but not necessarily another bird. If you buy a single

*Your single
Quaker will come
to rely on you for
affection and
companionship.*

bird, she will rely on you for attention. You will become the flock for this busy, funny, sociable creature.

Quakers do not hide their feelings well; in fact, they don't hide them at all. If you can appreciate this quality, a Quaker's expressiveness makes her a joy to be with and to watch. To be the object of a Quaker's affection will give you an amazing amount of satisfaction and happiness, but at times, you may feel as if you have fallen into the trap of the consummate control freak.

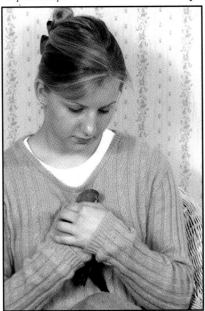

Quakers need a schedule, the more rigid the better. Food must be served at a certain time, time out of the cage must be permitted at a certain time (no cheating by cutting it short) and your bird will want time to interact with you every day. If you fail to follow the schedule, your Quaker is sure to let you know with words and other rule-breaking behavior.

Is a Quaker Right for You?

When choosing a bird, you should consider many factors, including those that might cause you, your family or your neighbors to wonder about the wisdom of your choice.

NOISE LEVEL

Whether you live in an apartment or a detached home, the potential noisiness of Quakers will be an important factor. Quakers call to one another and to their human companions using loud screeches. Some Quakers will be quieter than others, and hand-fed birds often fail to develop this loud screech. Some breeders hope to ensure that their birds will avoid learning to call loudly by separating them from aviaries of adults while they are too young to learn the behavior.

If harsh screeching sounds annoy you, a Quaker is probably not the ideal pet for you. Many Quaker owners and breeders are convinced that hand-fed birds are mostly quiet, sounding off only a few times a day. When it comes to assessing noise level, though, you must decide for yourself.

If you are unsure about the potential noise level of these birds, visit a breeder or pet store and observe the Quakers at several times of day for extended periods. In a pet store, ask store personnel about the noise. You might also consider taping Quaker calls and playing them at home.

If you plan to house several Quakers—a flock—outside or in a room with a wall that attaches to a neighbor's, noise will be a serious consideration. Quakers in a flock can be quite noisy. If you love the birds, the noise will seem inconsequential. A neighbor, on the other hand, may become annoyed, which can strain relations. If you plan to house your birds outside, always check local ordinances or deed restrictions *before* you build an aviary and buy birds.

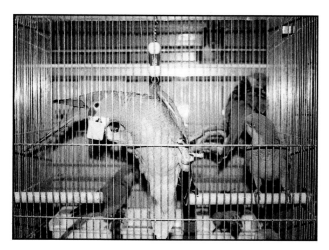

Before you buy a Quaker, visit a breeder or pet store to hear their potential noise level.

SIZE CONSIDERATION

Parrots come in many sizes, from the tiniest Pygmy parrots (genus *Mycropsitta*) to the largest Hyacinth Macaws (*Anodorhynchus hyacinthinus*). The larger the bird, the louder the noise and the more difficult it is to house her properly. The medium size of the Quaker makes her an ideal apartment or home dweller. Caging is relatively inexpensive and easy to find.

TIME COMMITMENT

How much time do you have to devote to an emotionally needy little bird? You should have at least several hours a day that you are willing to give to your bird for her care, both physical and emotional.

You should plan on spending at least two to three hours a day caring for your Quaker parrot.

BUDGETING FOR A PARROT

Cost is another important consideration when buying a bird. Because standard Quakers are bred successfully in the United States, hand-fed birds should be readily available at a reasonable cost. Green Quakers are among the most reasonably priced of pet parrots, especially when you consider their playful antics, innate sense of humor, talking ability and subtle beauty. If you have your heart set on a beautiful blue Quaker mutation, you will pay slightly more than double the price of a standard green bird. If you set your sights on a yellow, pied, cinnamon, albino or other rare mutation, you can expect to pay as much as twenty-two times the price of a standard bird—or more. Supply and demand are the rule of thumb in pricing birds.

ONE QUAKER MAY BE THE BEST CHOICE

Although Quaker parrots tolerate and sometimes do well with other birds, it is probably best to buy one as an only bird. When considering a Quaker, remember that wild Quaker parrots are relatively small creatures in a dangerous world. Those small animals that survive are often bold and aggressive. These qualities are inherited by hand-fed Quakers, too. This assertiveness means you will have to learn to train her to behave properly. Your obligation cannot be partial; you will have to demonstrate to your bird daily, in an acceptable way, that you are in charge and the house rules are in force. You must also understand and put into action positive behavior-modification techniques. Negative attention from you will only encourage a Quaker to misbehave.

Quakers are inquisitive and must be kept out of trouble with the attention of keen eyes.

CURIOUS BIRDS

Quaker parrots are busy birds. Wild Quakers chew branches and twigs to build large, intricate nests. This should be a clue to you that most of these birds will chew household items, even if they already have toys. Potential objects for chewing include jewelry, furniture, telephone and electrical wiring, baseboards and window treatments. You must be prepared to offer substitutes and be able to keep a wary eye on your Quaker's out-of-cage activities. This is not a bird you can keep in a cage all the time. You can circumvent damage by watching your bird and playing with her

25

while she is out and about. Examine your level of commitment.

ARE YOU A NEAT-FREAK?

How do you feel about messes? A Quaker parrot can be a never-ending source of clutter. If you don't mind cleaning feathers, dust, chewed wood and paper every-day to keep your bird healthy, then a Quaker might just be the bird for you! All birds are messy, but because Quakers are so active, they tend to spread disorder wherever they go. To take care of them is a labor of love. The payoff? A bird full of love and fun.

How to Choose a Quaker Parrot

By now you, too, may be charmed by Quakers—enough to want to add one to your family. But how do you choose the right bird? This and other questions probably swirl through your mind. My first, and per-haps most important, piece of advice is to look at as many Quaker parrots as possible. If they are legal to own in your state, look at pet stores, specialty bird stores and breeders.

At the first sight of a cage full of Quakers, you may fall in love with them all—as I did. The beautiful soft gray of the face and chest blends so exquisitely into the vivid green of the head and back. After taking all that in, you may notice the lovely indigo blue of the flight feathers and the pink-tinged beige beak. At about this time, you will begin to notice the bright glint in the eyes of each and every one of these be-witching little birds.

PERSONALITY PLUS

One of the most important things to remember about Quaker parrots, and any other bird, is that each will have her own personality. In general, they are outgo-ing, fun-loving, sometimes demanding birds. In partic-ular, each is different from the others. Spend some time with the bird you believe is the right one for you to learn if your personalities, needs and wants are compatible.

Visit as many of these sources as you can find in your area. Take the time to study a group of birds and handle them; you will soon find one with the personality for you. Do you want a cuddler? An independent bird? An energetic entertainer? List the qualities you want in an ideal avian companion and don't give up until you find a bird that has them all.

Each Quaker parrot has a unique, one-of-a-kind personality.

Make an Informed Purchase

Once you have decided to buy a Quaker parrot, avoid buying one on impulse. One of the secrets to buying the perfect bird is doing research and making careful observations, both of the bird and of the people selling it. The perfect bird will come from a clean establishment, whether that is a pet store, a hobby breeder or a professional breeder.

WHERE TO FIND A QUAKER PARROT

Pet stores are the logical first place to look for a pet. Take notes about the kinds of birds you find, the prices and the condition of the stores. Also note the helpfulness and knowledge of store personnel. Next, visit breeders. Both stores and breeders should be held to the same standards of cleanliness.

What to Look Out for

- Are the cages kept clean? Keep in mind that birds will pass droppings about every twenty minutes.

When you multiply that times the number of birds in the cage, you can see how the droppings will quickly add up. Accordingly, the cage bottom should be changed at least once a day.

- How clean are the perches? They should be free of droppings. Food and food containers must be spotless, and should always be located away from the birds' perching spots to prevent contamination from droppings. Water must be kept clean, without the addition of liquid vitamins or other supplements, which can spoil during the day. (Supplements often give the water a yellowish, oily appearance.) Only clean, clear water is acceptable.

- How many birds are kept in a cage? If there are too many, the birds will appear to be crowded and uncomfortable. Some may have been attacked; others may have chewed or pulled out their own feathers to reflect their stress. The cage housing too many birds may be overly dirty and the food soiled.

- Are the birds ever taken out for exercise and socialization?

- Who is allowed to handle the birds? Humans carry diseases on their skin, body hair and clothing. Anyone handling a bird should be required to wash with a disinfectant before doing so.

- What kind of diet are the birds fed? A balanced diet of seeds, fruits and vegetables will help ensure healthier birds than those fed only seed. Is the fresh food (fruits and vegetables) still appetizing? It should not remain in the cage long enough to spoil or grow mildew. Experienced birdkeepers remove fresh food after only a few hours. If it looks wilted or discolored, it should not be in the cage.

- Is the store or breeder's establishment clean in general? Where is food kept? Is it of high quality? Don't take a breeder's established reputation for granted. It's wise to check it out for yourself.

For more information, check with bird clubs in your area. Attend a few meetings and ask for recommendations on pet stores and breeders. People who belong to these clubs are friendly, interested in all birds and anxious to share information with others. This is a valuable resource, and it will cost you only the nominal dues if you decide to join. Ask club members for the name of an avian veterinarian in your area. Make an appointment and ask the vet to recommend pet stores, breeders and other sources for Quaker parrots. It is appropriate to pay for this visit—a veterinarian's time is valuable. Do not call a vet's office for free information.

Helpful pet store personnel should be able to answer your questions about Quaker parrots.

Information You Should Know About Your Quaker

PARENTS

With a Quaker parrot, it is important to learn about the bird's parents. What is their temperament? Sweet? Fun loving? Easy going? Intense? These traits are passed along to chicks and are important. Just as children may exhibit markedly different traits as adults than they did as young children, Quaker adults may be entirely different than very young birds. Genes help determine adult personalities.

AGE

The next consideration should be the age of the bird. Young birds are easier to tame than older birds. Ideally, the best bird is one that was hand-fed: A person, rather than her parents, fed her as a baby. This method familiarizes the bird with humans and teaches the bird to trust them. A hand-fed bird should bond to you as she did to her feeder. This doesn't mean you will not have to work with your bird to achieve a great relationship. It means that you and your bird will have a much easier time establishing your connection. I believe Quakers that have been pulled from their parents' nest as soon as they hatch and fed by humans have the best pet potential.

Eight weeks old is the ideal age to adopt a Quaker parrot—after she is weaned from hand-feeding.

You will want a bird that is about eight weeks old—weaned from hand-feeding formula. If she is not already weaned and eating regular food, that will become your job. Although some people want to do this and some also want to take over the hand-feeding of their new baby Quaker, I do not recommend it. Even for experienced birdkeepers, hand-feeding and weaning are time-consuming, anxiety-inducing activities.

In addition to being more trustful, hand-fed birds are often less noisy than parent-raised birds. Perhaps best of all, many of them like to cuddle, especially if they were handled often and lovingly by their caregivers while they were young chicks. Still, a Quaker will cuddle when and where she wants to—not always when you want to. These are independent birds, which is an intrinsic part of their charm.

Was She Hand-Fed?

In a perfect world, hand-feeding means that someone takes the time to feed, either with a spoon or a syringe, each chick clean, warm, nutritious formula, every two hours during the first few weeks of life, then every three hours when the chick was a bit older and so on, twenty-four hours a day. Hand-feeding continues until she is ready to be introduced to and convinced to eat the diet of an adult bird. As this ideal hand-feeder cares for the bird, she or he talks lovingly to the bird and strokes her to help her get used to humans—even to want and seek human companionship and close physical contact, such as snuggling.

How can you tell the difference between a bird that was lovingly nurtured and one that was not? When you choose a Quaker parrot, ask to hold her on your hand or finger. If she shies away from you in fright, she was probably not hand-fed properly and will need extensive training to learn to trust and want to be near humans. If she seems confident enough to step onto your finger or shoulder, she was hand-fed properly. You can tame a hand-shy bird, but be prepared for a large commitment of time and patience.

> ## WHAT DOES A HEALTHY BIRD LOOK LIKE?
>
> Stand back and look at all of the birds in the cage. It's time to find a healthy bird. Healthy birds have clear, bright eyes. Their nostrils are clear and their beaks are of normal length and have clean, sharp edges. Feathers are in good condition—not chewed or frayed. Those under the bird's tail (called the vent) should be clean and unstained. Diarrhea causes stains on the vent feathers; normal droppings will not stain the vent feathers. A healthy bird is free of cuts and abrasions. She sleeps with one foot up, balancing on the other foot.

Is She Healthy?

Once you have the bird out of the cage, run your finger gently down her chest. Healthy baby birds are nice and plump. They grow and gain weight quickly, soon outweighing their parents with the extra fat necessary for weaning. The chest should feel firm and full, the keel bone down the center of the chest should not feel sharp or stand out, which would indicate an underweight, or perhaps sick, bird.

Look carefully at the bird's feathers. She should have no bald spots. Some birds pull out their feathers; this may be a sign of frustration and unhappiness or a lack of opportunity to bathe often. Feather picking can become a hard-to-break habit. Her feathers should be clean and smooth. Both wings should hang evenly. The bird's grip on your fingers should be firm. The bird's breathing should be slow and even. A newly weaned bird may not have all of her feathers grown in. Pin feathers (growing feathers) look similar to aglets on the ends of shoelaces. Each feather is encased in a semi-opaque sheath. In the shaft of a new feather, you can see the blood source. Pin feathers should be clean of all formula or food. Look carefully at the feathers around the face and on the abdomen, where old, bacteria-laden food can become a health hazard.

**WHAT DOES AN
UNHEALTHY BIRD
LOOK LIKE?**

A sick bird is inactive for long periods of time. She may sit on the floor of the cage if she is terribly ill. Unhealthy birds may puff their feathers to keep warm, and they tend to sit on both feet. Fluffed birds look appealing, but should be avoided at all costs. Sick birds may have runny, dull-looking eyes and/or clogged nostrils. Their breathing may be wheezy and labored if they have respiratory problems. If there are a lot of sick birds in a cage, avoid buying any from that group.

Check the bird you want to buy at different times of the day to be sure she is active and healthy. Birds rest periodically, typically after meals, in the afternoon and in the late evening. But in between, a healthy Quaker should play with toys, look for mischief to get into and interact with others in her cage.

Birds do not exhibit obvious signs of illness until they are extremely ill. This trait serves them well in the wild, where predators single out sick animals as easy targets. In fact, a sick bird may be driven out of the flock by her own species because of the danger she brings to the group by attracting predators. Life in the wild is hard. Survival depends on such seemingly cruel practices. It is only when a bird is too ill to put forth the energy to disguise her state of health that she shows outward signs of illness. If a bird is that sick, do not buy her. She probably cannot be saved.

This may seem like a tremendous amount of information to take in and use to evaluate a bird. As you look at birds, though, you will begin to pick out the sick from the well, the hand-fed and tame from those still untamed. It will be easier if you can remember to look at the cage and the food, then the bird from head to toe. There will be fewer sick birds than well ones; unhealthy birds should stand out. The more you look, the easier it will become, particularly if you compare the photos of healthy birds in this book to the birds you see.

If you have a preference, such as for a talking bird, an especially active bird, a quiet bird or any other partiality, it's best to talk with the store owner or bird handler or with a breeder or the person who hand-fed the clutch you are looking at. These people should know the birds well and be able to guide you. Keep in mind, however, that younger chicks may change their personalities somewhat as they grow older. An experienced hand-feeder, bird handler or breeder should be able to help you by discussing such possibilities.

Make sure that your bird has been fed a balanced diet of seeds, fruits and vegetables.

Buying a Quaker parrot, or any bird, should be a time-consuming activity. If you rush it, you are more likely to bring home the wrong bird.

A Second-Hand Bird?

Sometimes people buy birds and find that they cannot keep them for various reasons, such as a decline in their own health, or a move to a state that prohibits the birds. Perhaps a friend or neighbor has noticed your

33

interest in his bird and has asked if you would like to "adopt" it.

If the bird is healthy and tame, why not? In such transactions, the bird usually comes with a cage, toys, dishes and other accessories. I know of many instances in which birds are much happier with their new owners, particularly if their former owners were unable to offer the love, time, security and nutrition the birds needed.

One Bird or Two?

The temptation for first-time bird owners is to buy two birds. If you buy two birds, they will bond to each other and seek their needed companionship from each other—even if they were hand-fed. They will tolerate you and may even interact with you, but the bond will not be as strong as it would have been had you bought only one bird. Sometimes, though, people buy two birds first, and then find that the birds will not bond to them, but only want to snuggle contentedly with each other. Separating birds that have bonded to each other is cruel. Don't consider it.

If you are considering a second bird, keep in mind that Quakers get along best with other Quakers.

On the other hand, if you buy only one bird, you will need to offer her the attention another bird or the birds in a colony would have given her. This doesn't mean twenty-four-hour-a-day tending; it means you will have to pay a reasonable amount of attention to the bird at set times (and set periods of time) each day. She will need lots of playtime out of the cage with toys and with you. You will find that she wants to cuddle and chatter at you, perhaps even tell you how she feels about various situations (in your language)—I can certainly think of many less enjoyable activities.

If you decide to buy two birds, both should be Quakers. Keeping two different species together could result in the death or injury of one of the birds.

Living

with a

part two

Quaker Parrot

Setting Up Your Quaker Parrot's Home

Quaker parrots thrive on activity. They need to run around, climb, chew and play constantly—certainly much more than is the norm for many larger birds. Their size makes this need relatively easy to accommodate.

Choosing the Cage

Before you buy your bird, buy his cage. Choosing the cage should take as much time as selecting the bird. This will be your bird's home. Check all available supply sources, including pet stores, feed stores and specialty builders that advertise in bird magazines. The guidelines are relatively simple and are based on the physical and emotional needs of Quaker parrots as well as their typical behaviors.

The cage size will, of course, first depend on your budget and the size of your home. Keep in mind that Quaker parrots are active and love to play and climb. They need this exercise for both their physical and mental well-being. Knowing this, choose the largest cage that you can afford. Ask pet store personnel to show you cages designed specifically for Quakers or cockatiels.

Caging needs for a Quaker vary depending on how much time he will spend in his cage. At the very least, the cage you choose should be the size of a large cage built for cockatiels. Your bird should have plenty of room to stretch his wings and to flap them whenever he feels the need for a little exercise. The cage must also be large enough to accommodate the huge number of toys your Quaker will need to keep his mind and body occupied while in his cage.

Decide where in your home you will place the cage. Make sure to allocate space for furniture. You will want to keep the Quaker's cage about 2 feet from any furniture; this will help prevent some wanton destruction. Avoid placing the cage near any irreplaceable furniture, books or window treatments. These guys have busy beaks and never ignore an object of potential affection and fun.

Your Quaker's cage should have plenty of room for stretching and exercise.

The cage must have bars close enough together to prevent the bird from squeezing its head and body through: about ⅜ inch. Take a tape measure with you to check the height and width (at least 18 inches by 18 inches), as well as the width of the bars.

39

EXTERIOR DESIGN

As you might imagine, a playpen built onto a cage is a great idea for these active clowns. One that opens from the top is optimal. The cage top looks flat until you unsnap the end portions and open it, fitting in special perches that hold the top open and form a place for the bird to sit. This is far preferable to a cage with a solid top serving as the permanent base of a play-ground. The solid base makes the cage too dark and is difficult to keep clean, an important consideration. On the other hand, a separate play gym is portable, inexpensive and will allow your bird plenty of exercise.

A built-on playpen saves space while providing a fun place to exercise.

Horizontal cage bars are best, with some vertical bars in between to act as framing. The horizontal bars will encourage necessary climbing activity. Bars should be relatively close together to prevent escapes. More importantly, the close bars will help prevent your bird from getting his head stuck between the bars, which could result in severe injury or death.

As you look at cages, you will see that those designed for big parrots have larger perches and bars spaced more widely apart—making it easy for a Quaker parrot to climb right through! Avoid cages for budgies because they are too small.

Ornate cages are beautiful to look at, but they are also difficult to clean. Ornate cages can also have bits of metal that stick out decoratively, but which can catch a bird's foot, wing, beak or leg band, causing injury or death.

The cage *must* be metal. Plastic, bamboo and wooden cages sold for finches are beautiful, but are no match for a Quaker's strong beak. Your bird would be out in a flash. The kind of metal you choose is of utmost importance, too.

Easy to Clean?

Choose a cage that will clean easily, such as those made of chrome or stainless steel. Some metal cages come in an array of powder-coated paint colors that are attractive and easily cleaned. To avoid the dangers of lead-based paint, make sure that any cages with a

Your best bet is a chrome or stainless-steel cage that will be easy to clean.

powder coating were manufactured in the United States or Canada. Cages made in Mexico are especially likely to present lead problems, both in paint and in the metal and welded joints. Avoid metals that will discolor when exposed to the fruits and vegetables your bird will throw as he eats or will wipe on the bars to keep his beak clean.

Plastic-coated metal bars can look attractive, but are unsuitable: Your bird will spend many hours stripping the plastic off the bars. While this may be fun for your bird, you will not enjoy the sight or the mess.

Because keeping your bird's cage clean is important, choose one that will be easy to work on. If it's too complicated, you will be less likely to clean the cage daily, and failure to do so will compromise your bird's health.

The Cage Tray

The easiest design is one with a built-in tray in the bottom of the cage. This slides out, so you can remove the soiled paper and throw it away, replacing it with fresh. The drawer should be tall enough to contain the litter as you pull it out, and should slide easily. A wire bottom should separate the bird from the refuse in the tray by 3 inches or so. Another easy-to-handle style has a snap-on bottom. To clean this, you simply place remove the bottom, placing the cage on newspapers while you work.

Your Quaker's cage should have a wire bottom that separates the bird from the cage tray by about 3 inches.

THE CAGE DOOR

Cage doors come in four basic designs: those that open to the side; those that slide to the side; those that slide up, leaving an open square and those that open from top to bottom, forming a porch for a bird to play on. The only door style I tend to avoid is the one that slides up to open. This door has to be secured while open, and if your curious Quaker plays with the latch, the door will slide shut with a bang, something like a guillotine.

Accessories

The following is a list of items that will make your life easier and will help you keep your Quaker parrot happy and healthy.

DEBRIS CONTAINERS

All that activity in a Quaker parrot cage kicks up a lot of feathers, seed hulls, bird droppings, fruit and vegetable scraps and toy parts. The busy day-to-day living of these extroverts can get messy. Fortunately, some old-fashioned and some new-fangled equipment helps contain this debris in the cage. Which you choose will depend as much on price as appearance.

The simple, elasticized cloth "skirt" has been around for ages. You can choose this style in a variety of materials to match your home. It is washable and inexpensive, but Quakers chew anything they can get hold of, so you should plan on replacing this as needed. If you sew, the expense will be minimal, but the mess involved might be more than you really want to deal with. All of my birds seem to relish the feel of cloth in their beaks and enjoy the sound it makes as they tear it.

Other seed guards are made of plastic or metal. Some cages come with 3-to-4-inch-high plastic inserts around the edges of the cage. These will work well if they are made of sturdy plastic that will hold up against strong

A cage with a wide apron to catch debris will cut down cleaning time.

beaks. Glass guards are also available, or you can have them cut for a reasonable price at a glass shop to replace any thin plastic guards that came with the cage.

Some more expensive cages come with a wide apron that flares out from the base of the cage. This is an effective way to catch the debris. You may also find aprons sold alone to attach to cages.

The ultimate in mess containment is an acrylic or glass cage or flight. Although you may find either at your local pet store, it is more often a special-order item found in bird magazine advertisements or at bird marts.

DISHES

Your bird will need at least two feeding dishes and two water dishes. All must be made of ceramic or stainless steel; Quakers have strong beaks and will gleefully destroy any others.

If the cage you have chosen doesn't have four dishes built in, you can buy extras to hang on the cage sides. If this is the case, try them out in the store to make sure they hang correctly and can be positioned away from the perches, where the bird might soil their contents with droppings.

Ceramic or stainless-steel feeding dishes should hold up to your Quaker's strong beak.

A relatively new feeding dish on the market bolts to the side of the cage with a wing nut outside the cage. (This is an important feature. Quakers are intelligent birds and would soon unscrew any readily available nut or bolt, thereby dumping the dish.) Although the initial price seems high, it is definitely worth it because these dishes will last many years.

WATER BOTTLES

Perhaps the best solution for water is a bottle made for the purpose, which you can hang outside the cage. A ball-bearing prevents the water from leaking. When the bird touches the ball with his tongue, a drop of water comes out. The biggest advantage of a water bottle is that the bird's droppings and old food will not fall into it. Anything organic that falls into the water is likely to grow bacteria—and that can cause your bird to get sick.

WHERE TO BATHE?

If you offer your bird water in a bottle, you must also provide a wide, shallow dish for your Quaker to bathe in every day, preferably outside the cage on his T-stand or play gym. For Quakers, bathing is not a luxury, it is a daily necessity to feel physically and emotionally healthy. Some cages have extra openings with doors that swing out of the way. This allows you to hang a cockatiel-size bath on the outside of the cage, flush to the cage wall, and gives the bird free access to the bath from inside his cage. This style of bath is easy to keep clean because it is less likely to become fouled by droppings or food than a dish on the bottom of the cage. The bath you buy should fit well enough that your bird cannot escape through any gaps.

Using a water bottle is a good way to keep your Quaker's water clean.

Whatever style of dishes you choose, be sure to have at least one extra set on hand. I like to have four complete sets for each of my bird cages. That way, I always have a set of clean dishes to put in my birds' cages every morning—even if I have not run the dishwasher in a day or two.

PERCHES

The cage you choose will come with perches. More than likely, they will be wooden or plastic dowels. Plastic perches are unacceptable, so if the cage is otherwise perfect, replace them. Replacement perches are usually inexpensive, and buying the correct perches is one of the most important purchases you will make for your bird's home.

45

In the wild, birds land on a variety of branches, leaves, rocks and other natural material. They climb and they walk, which exercises their feet. They rest with one foot on the perch and one pulled up in their feathers. The variety of perching material they use helps ensure healthy feet and nails. This is essential, whether the bird is wild or a pet. Except while they fly, birds are always on their feet—even when asleep. Exercising their feet on perches of a variety of shapes and sizes helps keep circulation efficient and feet in good shape.

The bird should not be able to wrap his feet all the way around the smallest part of the perch; on the other hand, the perch should not be so large that the bird cannot grip it firmly. Perches should be labeled for specific bird species or sizes.

Most pet stores carry perches of such natural material as manzanita and other woods, as well as dried cholla cactus skeletons. As you look at them, you will notice that the branches vary in width and have interesting twigs that your bird will enjoy chewing, and bark that he can strip. Avoid sandpaper-covered perches and sandpaper designed to slip over perches: They can rub your Quaker's feet raw.

Vary the shapes and sizes of your Quaker's perches to keep his feet healthy.

As you look at the wooden perches, you may wonder if they are a waste of money. Your Quaker will gleefully chew any wood until it is sawdust. Chewing is a necessary and natural activity for parrots of any size. It gives them something interesting to do and it keeps their beaks in the correct shape. Wild Quakers chew branches and twigs to get them ready to weave into a nest. Those instincts remain in pet Quakers, including hand-fed birds.

A parrot's beak grows throughout his life, and chewing keeps the beak trimmed and conditioned for splitting seeds and nuts. Perches are an important part of a bird's environment. Wooden perches are well worth the expense.

Position several perches high in the cage. Quakers feel most secure when they can sit toward the top of the cage, especially when they rest. Be sure to allow enough room for your bird to sit straight, without ducking, on those high perches, and place the perches far enough from the cage walls that he won't hit his tail. Be sure to locate some perches near food dishes or cups.

Floor Coverings

Wild birds lose feathers as they fly, bathe and groom themselves (preen). They throw food as they eat and play. Their droppings fall to the ground unnoticed by them, where they are recycled and help to revitalize the earth.

A pet bird continues these activities, but the debris collects on the bottom of his cage, where it can grow mold, fungus and bacteria if not attended to regularly. This means the floor of the cage must be covered with something to help you keep the bird's environment as clean as possible, as easily as possible.

A variety of products is on the market for this purpose, including sanitized bird sand, gravel-covered paper, ground corn cobs or walnut shells and other bedding material. Of them all, I prefer black and white newspaper. I have it on hand, it's nontoxic and incurs no additional expense. (Do not use pages printed with colored inks, however. They can be toxic to your bird.)

Toys, Wonderful Toys

With toys, just about anything goes, with some guidelines to protect your bird. In his zeal to have fun, your

bird will not know a toy is dangerous—that is your job.
There are still too many hazardous toys on the market.

Look for toys made of natural, untreated and un-
painted wood. Quaker parrots (and most other healthy
parrots) chew. The best toy, in the view of a Quaker,
is one that can be thoroughly played with and
destroyed. This gives the bird intellectual and physical
exercise. Quakers, perhaps more than any other parrot, love playing with toys. You will need lots of toys
for the cage, and many
more so you can rotate
toys at least once a week.

*Quakers love to
play with toys,
especially ones
that they can
chew.*

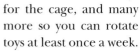

Hanging toys of natural,
specially treated leather
are fun for Quakers to
chew. The texture is dif-
ferent than wood and
holds their interest.
Some toys combine nat-
ural wood with knotted
leather. Other great toys
are made of cholla cactus, wooden beads and other
wooden shapes, such as teddy bears, chili peppers,
dinosaurs, cats and people.

Safety First

Avoid snap locks that are sometimes used to attach
a toy to the top of a cage. Birds tend to get toes, legs
and leg bands caught in these. If you aren't home
when this happens, your bird might lose a foot, a
leg or his life. If you like the toy, remove the snap
attachment and replace it with a stainless-steel or aluminum quick-link that attaches to the cage with a
nut-and-bolt–style closure. Quick-links are available at
hardware stores.

Birds are also in danger from toys with chains whose
links contain spaces. If a bird catches a body part, he
will panic and thrash around, injuring himself.

Occasionally you will see bird toys suspended from slip-
on key rings. Just as keys slide easily into the groove to

glide onto the ring, so can bird toes and beaks. Please replace any that are on toys you buy with quick-links.

Avoid thin plastic toys. Quakers will chew them and break the plastic into dangerous little pieces. Toys made of heavy acrylic are fine, and those made of brightly colored pieces of moveable acrylic will entertain Quakers. These birds are bright enough to enjoy toys that can be opened by taking off wing nuts or can be manipulated to hide peanuts and other treats. An intellectually challenging toy is perfect for nimble Quaker brains.

Play Gyms

One toy you will find indispensable is a play gym for medium-size parrots. This should come with at least one perch. It may also have a ladder and swing. It will sit on a base to catch any droppings. If you can afford one that sits on its own stand, so much the better. Be sure, however, that the perch is no higher than the middle of your chest or the chest of the smallest person who will handle the bird. This will help prevent your bird from deciding he is dominant over any human in the household.

Your Quaker's play gym should be fun, safe and stimulating.

The best rule of thumb for buying a toy, free-standing perch or play gym? If it looks dangerous, don't buy it. Look for protruding metal pieces, open spaces that could catch a small body part and anything that snaps. All of these pose potential problems.

Supplies to Avoid

When you look at supplies for your bird's cage you will see some items that are inappropriate, even though widely sold. Pet birds rarely have mites, making mite protectors an unnecessary accessory. More important, these protectors contain dangerous chemicals to which your bird should not be exposed. If someone tells you that your bird has mites, take the bird to a veterinarian for expert advice.

SAYING GOOD NIGHT

Your Quaker parrot will need a cage cover. Whether you buy it or make it, this is a necessary but simple accessory. A cage cover serves several purposes. Foremost, it gives your bird a sense of security during the night, a time a bird instinctively feels vulnerable. The temperature in most homes drops at night, especially in winter. A cage cover will help protect your bird from drafts and sudden temperature changes that can stress him.

From your standpoint, the best reason for a cage cover may be to keep your bird quiet in the morning. Instinctively, many birds begin calling out to flock members (you) at dawn. You may think you can outlast or ignore an insistent Quaker calling your name, but you'll be wrong on both counts. If you, like me, prefer getting up a bit later than sunrise, a cage cover will help you achieve that goal. A cage cover can be made out of a loosely woven piece of cloth, a large sheet towel or a beach towel.

Placing your Quaker's cage next to an inside wall will give him a sense of security.

Cage Placement

Where you put the cage in your home is as important as the cage itself. Quakers are social creatures. Like all birds, they feel best when they are members of a flock. You will become the bird's flock when you bring him home with you. Place the cage in a room where you spend a great deal of your leisure time, such as the family room.

The best place to locate the cage is next to an inside wall, so the bird doesn't have to worry about constant, unpredictable activity all around his home. Outside walls—those that face the outside of the house—can become too cold if you live in an area that has harsh winters. Interior walls are always a better bet for temperature control. Placing the cage near a wall will help calm your bird and give him some much-needed security. If you can, place the cage in a corner to give it two solid sides.

The cage top should be at about your chest height. You can place the cage on a sturdy four-legged table, or you can hang it from the ceiling. Old-fashioned stands made to hang cages are generally unsuitable because they can be tipped over easily.

A room with enough windows to let in plenty of natural light is ideal, although you should avoid putting the cage directly in front of a window, where direct sunlight could overheat your bird.

chapter 5

Bringing
Your Bird
Home

Before you leave the establishment that sold you your bird, ask that the bird's wings be clipped. If store personnel are not able to do this, ask your avian vet to do the job. Not only is this necessary for your peace of mind, but you will not want your bird loose where she may not be able to fend for herself. Another argument for keeping a Quaker's wings clipped is that we must earn the trust of agricultural interests in North America. Responsible owners clip their bird's wings to help prevent escapes, which result in recriminations from those who would ban Quakers from all states.

The Trip Home

Bring home your new bird in a secure container. Quakers chew energetically; a cardboard box will not contain her for long. It would be best to use a strong travel cage made of heavy stainless steel, aluminum wire or acrylic. A secure travel cage will also help your bird feel more protected in a situation that can only be frightening at best. This may, after all, be her first trip in a car.

As you travel, keep her out of drafts, including those from the auto air-conditioning or windows. If it's winter, avoid overheating your bird in the car, only to expose her to harsh weather when you leave the car. If the weather is wet or cold, cover the travel cage with a waterproof cover, towel or blanket. I prefer to use cage coverings that are the same color as the bird in question. Following this line of thinking, a soft gray or green covering might be soothing to your bird.

First, Visit the Veterinarian

Avoid taking children or other pets in the car on your trip to pick up the bird. Wherever you buy her, talk to her calmly and quietly from the moment you come into contact with her. Continue this pattern all the way to your avian veterinarian's office for your bird's first, and most necessary, physical exam. Also, if you have any questions about handling your bird, your avian veterinarian can demonstrate during this visit. If the bird's wings have not already been clipped, ask your vet to do so. Be sure the vet uses your towel for the restraint to avoid the use of any towel that might have been contaminated by previous use. (It may not seem likely, but I've seen towels used and reused in busy vets' offices.)

While the vet is trimming the wings, observe carefully so that you can carry out this procedure in the future, if necessary. Ask to be shown your bird's blood feathers. They have a distinct appearance; once you have seen one, you can easily recognize and avoid them. If you clip a blood feather, the bird can quickly bleed to death unless you know how to apply first-aid techniques, such as pulling the feather properly or stanching the flow of blood. (See the first-aid section in chapter 8.)

Ask that both wings be clipped. If only one wing is clipped, the bird can still fly, but cannot fly straight

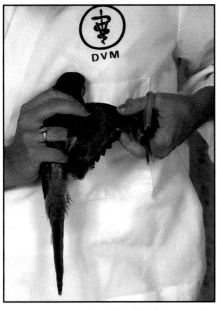

On the way home, stop at the veterinarian's office for a wing trim and check-up.

and is likely to get hurt as she tries to get away from you during training sessions. If you request it, the wings can be clipped so that the trimmed feathers do not show when the bird has her wings at her sides. This is not difficult to do, but may not occur to the vet if you don't mention it.

Clipping the wings will make your bird more dependent on you. She will recognize her altered state immediately, and she will be easier to train. Part of your obligation as an owner of a Quaker parrot is to keep her wings clipped throughout her life. Within your home, clipped wings will help prevent your bird from serious injury on mirrors, windows, ceiling fans and other dangers. It will also help prevent escape and all of the implications of escape, for the bird, for you and for agricultural concerns.

Adjustment Time

Keep in mind that your bird, although normally full of energy, daring and intelligent curiosity, will most certainly be exhausted, both physically and emotionally, by the time you arrive home. Because of the high level of stress the bird will have reached by that time, your household should be as soothing an environment as possible.

If you own a dog or cat, make sure she is kept away from the Quaker parrot until your bird is comfortable in her new home. This may take several days. Explain to any young children that they should speak quietly around the bird, avoiding any sudden movement and teasing behavior.

TRUST

The basis for taming a Quaker parrot is trust, and it will be up to you to establish that bond between you and your new feathered companion. Once that connection has been made, training should move along steadily.

You may be a bit afraid of your Quaker and her beak, so you will have to learn to trust your parrot, as well as your instincts for how she will react to certain situations. Until you get to know and love one another, you and your bird are strangers, and you have all the size, strength and familiarity with your surroundings on your side.

The temptation with any new bird is to bring her home and begin a training session immediately. This can undermine your Quaker's potential to trust you. Each bird is so different, the best method is to learn about your bird's personality before you make any rash assumptions and ruin your relationship before it starts.

Give your Quaker parrot plenty of time to get used to her new home.

If you arrive at home in the evening, put your bird in a cage with her toys, seed, pellets and water. Cover her for the night, but leave the lights on for an hour or so to let her become accustomed to her new home, then turn them off and let your bird get some rest for the full days ahead.

If you come home in the daytime, place your bird in her cage and allow her to get used to her new home,

55

play with her toys and sample the food in her dishes. If you are afraid to handle the bird, put the door of her traveling cage next to the door of her cage and allow her to jump into her new home on her own.

Taming and Training

When handling your Quaker, keep a soothing tone of voice and a calm demeanor.

If your bird was hand-fed and will accept handling by a stranger (you), gently cup her body in your right hand: Place your hand, palm-side down, over the bird's body with your thumb on her left wing and the rest of your fingers on her right wing. Gently grasp the bird and slowly move her from one cage to another. *Never*

wear gloves when working with a bird. Most birds find human hands frightening to some degree, and gloves will only magnify her alarm over her new situation.

If the bird bites you, you must not react by dropping her or making a loud noise. Quaker parrots are intelligent and easily make the connection in a cause-and-effect situation. No matter what happens during this transfer and later training, you must remain calm, talking to the bird in a low, quiet voice full of affection, using her name often. If you are prepared for the worst—a nasty bite—you will be able to react appropriately. I speak from experience: I've tamed and trained three wild-caught birds that were terrified initially. It soon was apparent that they were far more nervous than I was. After all, I knew what was about to happen; they did not.

Getting Started

Leave your bird alone for an hour or so with soft music playing. At the end of that time, you may sit a few feet away, talking in a low, soothing, calm voice. Use her name often, no matter what you say, so the bird can become used to the sound. Stay there for no longer than about fifteen minutes. Offer the bird a treat as you leave by placing it in a dish. You may give her a grape, a piece of apple or a small piece of a millet sprig. This will help your bird associate you with good things.

In thirty minutes or so, come back and sit again, repeating your efforts. This will allow your bird to observe you and get used to you at the same time you are getting a sense of her personality. If she appears unafraid, you may work at a faster rate.

Continue normal activity. Talk to your bird often in a quiet voice, using her name frequently. Put your hands in or on the cage as little as possible, except during cleaning sessions and when offering treats. Parrots regard their cages as their territory, and a pet Quaker parrot can become particularly vehement about her belongings.

TRAINING EQUIPMENT

Before you begin training your bird, assemble the necessary equipment. You should have on hand a wooden dowel-type perch, your bird's play gym or T-stand and some millet and sunflower seeds.

I know trainers who recommend gloves, but using gloves will only make it more difficult, if not impossible, for your bird to feel sure that your intentions are good. Even birds that have never seen gloves fear them; they have a difficult enough time with bare hands. As a novice, I even tried flesh-colored, close-fitting gloves to train a wild-caught bird. I was not only unsuccessful, but the use of the gloves set back our training by several days, at least.

If your bird bites you and will not let go, place your thumb and forefinger on opposite sides of her beak, on the skin where the upper mandible meets the lower mandible. Press gently on this area with your fingers. The bird should release her grip. If she does not, pry her beak apart with both fingers. Put the bird on her perch and begin again.

A SPECIAL PLACE TO TRAIN

Next, choose a room in which you will work with your bird each day. It should be small and contain few pieces of furniture and no knickknacks. I prefer the bathroom for training, because it meets these qualifications.

If you use the bathroom, close off the bathtub and shower, if you will not use them for training, and shut the toilet lid. Cover any furniture in the room with drop cloths, cover windows and mirrors and close any doors. If you use a room with a fireplace, close the flue (opening) so the bird cannot fly up the chimney. Remove or hide all electric cords. If you are working in a room without carpet, put a blanket or quilt on the floor to cushion the bird's crash landings. Perhaps the best place to train is inside a shower stall that is large enough for you to sit in on a soft mat or blanket.

Some birds will come out of the cage on their own with some gentle encouragement.

THE TRAINING SESSION

For this all-important first session with your bird, wear a neutral color. The best colors would include gray, green and soft blue, similar to your Quaker's feathers. This choice of clothing will help your bird remain calm. Bright colors, on the other hand, might frighten her or cause her to become overly excited. An agitated bird may be more prone to bite, and certainly more difficult to train. Particularly at this moment, you will want to appear as friendly and appealing as possible—nothing like a predator might look.

Bring your bird's cage into the training room with a clock, the perch or play gym, a dowel perch and treat seeds. To avoid exhausting the bird—and possibly your patience—the actual working part of the session should not last more than fifteen minutes. Work alone, without other people or animals around.

"STEP UP!"

Place the cage on the floor and sit down on the floor several feet away. Talk quietly to the bird, calling her by name and allowing her to get used to her surroundings. When she seems more relaxed, open the door to her cage. Gripping one end of the dowel perch, slide it slowly into the cage as you continue to talk to your bird. Put the perch under the curve of the bird's abdomen, just above her legs. Push up and in (gently but firmly); this will put your bird a bit off balance, forcing her to step up and onto the perch. As you are doing this, say, "Step up!" Pull the bird and perch out of the cage to begin the session.

This Quaker parrot is learning to "Step up!"

If this method does not work, open the cage door and allow the bird to come out on her own. You can tempt her with treats, then sit quietly and wait for her to come out of her cage. Next, push the dowel up under her abdomen to encourage her to step on it. Just as she begins to step onto the perch, say, "Step up!" Watch

59

the bird. She may pull the dowel toward her body to adjust the distance she must bridge to climb on. She may also "taste" the perch before she climbs on, "beaking" it gently. Observing this will help you discriminate between a bite, which will be quick, hard and painful, and this more harmless behavior.

Once the bird is on the dowel, move her toward you *slowly*, keeping the bird chest high. Talk to her gently, in a reassuring manner. In a few minutes, when you are ready to put her back on her cage for a rest, say, "Step down!" Using these commands consistently will give your bird a sense of security; she will know exactly what you expect of her and when. These commands also indicate that you are the leader of the flock, a position you must assume when you buy your bird.

If your bird flutters away, don't chase her with the dowel. Let her sit on the floor until she becomes more calm. Move toward her, still sitting, not standing. Attempt to get her to step up on the dowel again. Put her on the play gym or cage top. Sit nearby, talking in a pleasant voice, calling your bird by name. When the bird seems more composed, encourage her to climb on the dowel again. Repeat the "Step up!" command. End the session fifteen to twenty minutes after actual work on the dowel begins. Never grab her or use a net. Grabbing will scare your bird and set back the training schedule. Netting a bird can result in injury, panic and, worst of all, loss of trust.

During the next session, repeat your actions. After the bird responds to the command and the gentle nudge by getting on the dowel, it's time to teach her to step onto your hand. To do this, squeeze all fingers together, as you hold your hand in a horizontal position, thumb tucked tight to the hand. As the bird sits on the dowel or on her play gym, push your hand up under her abdomen, to gently push the bird off balance. As she steps onto your hand, say "Step up!" If she seems a bit panicked, your bird may accept your hand cupped protectively over her back or in front of her face. To get your hand in position, move slowly. If the sight of your hand coming toward her makes her more anxious, slowly move the hand away, in full sight of the bird.

When your bird readily steps onto your hand, she is exhibiting her trust in you. Every time you work with your bird, you must act only in a trustworthy manner, at the same time exhibiting the confidence and calm manner a bird might expect from a leader of the flock. You must earn your bird's trust and respect every day.

Work Slowly, Reward Often

Talk to your bird as you work, and offer some millet or a sunflower seed, if you wish. A tiny bit of peanut butter on your finger or hand might tempt even the wariest bird. If that's what tempted your Quaker parrot to step onto your hand, give her time to eat some before you continue the session.

Always move slowly as you work with your bird. End each session about fifteen minutes after it began. If your bird was hand-fed and is still young, she will tame in a short period of time; it's difficult to predict exactly how long it will take. That can depend on your personality, your bird's personality and experience with other humans, whether she was hand-fed with care or parent-raised and how young she is.

After your bird has learned to "Step up!" slowly begin to train her to accept affection.

CUDDLING YOUR QUAKER

When your bird will step confidently onto your hand in response to the "Step up!" command, then you can begin to train her to accept petting, kissing and cuddling. This must all be done in the same unhurried manner as the early training. If you want to pet your bird, begin by touching her lower abdomen with one finger. She may bite, but after many sessions, your bird can learn to not only accept your touch, but to welcome it.

Petting her abdomen can be followed by petting her head. This may be more difficult. Many birds fear having a human's hand over their backs. If she was hand-fed, though, your bird was held by the breeder, who gently cupped the bird's head and back in one hand; a hand-fed bird will be used to this position. After your bird accepts petting, you can begin the sometimes slow process of teaching her to cuddle.

If you are working with a young bird, the training sessions will yield the desired results much sooner than if the bird is a wild-caught, feral chick or was parent-raised in a captive community. Such birds are still trainable, but it will take more patience and more time to accomplish the task. An older, feral Quaker or a bird that has been mistreated may not tame well at all.

Remember to give your Quaker several out-of-cage playtimes each day.

Dos and Don'ts

- Do set times to play with your Quaker every day.

- Do adhere to a schedule for feeding, playing and bathing your bird; this will allow her to feel secure. Even an hour longer than usual in her cage will seem interminable to your Quaker.

- Do take your bird out of her cage at least once a day. If you can only take her out once each day, make that a long playtime. A Quaker that spends too much time in her cage will soon become territorial, refusing to come out and interact with anyone.

- Do carry your bird to several play sites each day, including a play gym, a swing or a free-standing perch. Watch for signs that she wants to move to another location. Moving your bird several times while she plays outside her cage will also help prevent her from becoming too possessive of her cage.

- Do offer a wide variety of toys, and change them often so your bird does not become overly possessive of the toys or their positions in the cage. Moving the toys and perches can give the cage a new look, also a help in preventing territoriality.

- Do say "Step up!" each time you offer your bird your hand, your arm or a dowel to get on.

- Do demonstrate to others in the house the proper way to handle the bird to encourage her trust and respect.

- Don't allow your bird to sit anywhere higher than your chest height.

HEIGHT ADVICE

Several years ago, avian behaviorist Sally Blanchard began dispensing some unique advice: Don't let your bird sit on your shoulder or on anything tall enough that her eyes will be as high as your own. Sally noticed that parrots with cocky personalities, such as Quakers, are more aggressive if they view themselves on a physical par with the humans in their lives.

After hearing Sally talk on the subject, I began to look at my own birds, some of whom had taken control of our home. It became obvious that some of their worst misbehavior took place when they were either on my shoulder or on a tall piece of furniture. Take her advice to heart. Keep your bird elevated no higher than your chest height, where her eyes will not be higher than your own.

- Don't allow your bird to sit on your shoulder.

- Don't allow your bird to exhibit aggressive behavior, including biting or chasing. A five-minute time out in a quiet place away from people may be called for if this kind of behavior occurs.

- Don't allow your bird to roam the house at will. She may become territorial about the house and may destroy anything in her path. She may also endanger herself by chewing on electric cords or other dangerous household items.

- Don't shout at or hit the bird, no matter what has occurred. This may frighten your new pet, erode the trust you have earned and encourage aggressive behavior. Another possible result of shouting at a Quaker is that she will enjoy the excitement you have created and seek to re-create the situation by biting, screaming or whatever she had done originally that incited your response.

- Do cover your Quaker parrot's cage with a cloth of a neutral color when she becomes overly excited. This will give her time to calm down.

Potential Problems and How to Avoid Them

As might be expected with any intelligent creature, there is a real potential for behavioral problems with your Quaker parrot. The root of any such problem, though, can be traced to one source: *you.* As you train and work with your bird throughout her life, remember that you trained her. If you believe you do not have a strong enough personality to be the leader of the flock, a more docile parrot species might be a better choice.

BITING

Being bitten is probably the worst fear of new bird owners. Certainly a parrot's bite hurts, and may even create a deep cut. This is, however, the principal way a parrot has to show you that she is frightened, upset or excited, especially if she does not know you and has not been trained to understand what is acceptable and what is not.

How to Avoid a Bite

Never try to clean your bird's cage with the bird inside. Never try to take away a toy or remove a toy from the cage while your bird is still inside. This will agitate your bird and she may bite you. Take her into another room for a visit with someone else while you clean the cage. Lacking another person to play with, you could put your bird in her travel cage or on a T-stand or play gym with plenty of toys or treats to occupy her attention, while you clean up.

Avoid reaching into a cage to remove your Quaker parrot. Instead, open the door to invite her out. Use the "Step up!" command when she comes out of her cage to sit on the door or the top of the cage. When you put her down on her T-stand, play gym or the top of her cage, always give her a "Step down!" command so she knows what you expect and that you are in command.

Birds in the wild play rough and bite each other; always set limits when playing with your Quaker.

If the bird bit you during the normal range of acceptable training because she had become frightened or had been trying to establish herself as dominant, you can gently shake your arm, keeping it horizontal so the bird will lose her balance and sense of well-being, but will not fall off. This method has worked and still works for all of my trained birds. Even with clipped wings, any of my birds can keep her balance by flapping those wings, because I use my strength prudently. It's a gentle, harmless, but firm reminder that I am in control of the situation, and am still leader of the flock.

WARNING SIGNS

If you watch your bird carefully, you can see signs that a bite is imminent: feathers suddenly pulled in, eyes focused intently on a body part, a head pulled back slightly to allow a quick strike. Keep mental track of any bites or strikes, noting in particular the reason the bird lost her cool. This will prepare you for the future. If something you or someone else did caused the bite and can be avoided, avoid a repeat in the future.

TIME OUT

If a gentle shaking does not work, I recommend putting your Quaker in her cage for a five to ten minute time out. Keep your voice and movements calm. If your bird is especially agitated, you can cover her with a neutral-colored cloth for some quiet time. If possible, leave the room. The only noise should be some quiet music. This will allow the bird to see who is in control and to collect herself as she calms down. You can take this time to relax, as well. This method works especially well if your bird is overstimulated either by a toy or by playing with a member of your family, by sexual activity with a toy or by jealousy. After no more than ten minutes, you can uncover the cage. Longer periods of time are ineffective; the bird will have forgotten what occurred.

Socializing Your Quaker

Just as a Quaker parrot left too long in her cage may become possessive of her cage and toys, she may also become overly jealous and dangerously protective of a person who assumes sole or primary responsibility for her care. Not all Quakers will react this way, but you should take no chances. If you live with others or expect your bird to interact with others, you must help train her to accept and relate to other people.

It can be terribly flattering to have an animal who wants only to be with you. In the end, however, unless you live utterly alone and never have or want visitors, this will be an unhealthy relationship; it may become dangerous to anyone who expects to come near you and speak with you or take part in other normal activities of daily living with you.

Accomplishing the task of socializing your Quaker is not difficult, but will take diligence on your part. Shortly after your Quaker is hand-trained, begin introducing other members of your family, requiring that they learn to dispense and expect the same training routines that you have given the parrot. Frequent handling of the Quaker by these people will be required.

If the bird becomes so attached to you that she will not allow contact with anyone else, back off for as long as it takes your parrot to learn to trust others. Allow your family members to take over feeding and playing with the bird. Encourage them to offer treats whenever they are with the bird, a bit of a favorite seed or nut, a grape or a small piece of cheddar cheese. If you follow this plan diligently, your bird will learn to interact with all family members.

Certain situations will almost certainly cause a Quaker, and many other parrot species, to bite. Knowing in advance what these are can help you and your bird avoid painful and upsetting altercations. Keep in mind at all times that pet Quaker parrots are extremely intelligent and territorial. Put simply, they will defend vigorously what they believe they own. This includes their cage, particularly the inside of the cage, and toys.

Beware! Putting your Quaker on your shoulder may be cute, but it will also give her the wrong idea that she is in charge.

WHO'S IN CHARGE?

Avoid allowing your bird to sit where she might be higher than you are. This is a position of power from a Quaker parrot's point of view. Once in a position of power, your pet may feel compelled to keep you in line. Wild Quakers, especially adolescents, battle constantly to determine who will lead the group. This instinct is strong in many Quaker parrots and helps ensure survival of the species in the wild. When the most intelligent, aggressive bird is the leader of the flock, the whole group is more likely to find enough food and escape predators, carrying on the species. Your bird cannot fight these instincts, but you can help overcome her reactions by understanding them yourself.

If you are familiar with children, you will see a constant parallel in effective ways to handle children and Quaker parrots. Just as children sometimes have tantrums or become too tired to react rationally, Quakers sometimes become emotionally overwrought. If you see this happening, do not try to interfere until the moment has passed.

POINTING IS RUDE

Quaker parrots do not like to be pointed at. (Do you?) If you point at your Quaker parrot *and* raise your voice in rebuke, your pet may give you a nasty bite. Instead, keep your responses to any mischief low-key. It's up to you to set a calm tone.

If a visitor to your home wants to handle your Quaker, educate that person in how to pick up and put down your bird, using the commands and exhibiting self-confidence. Any hesitancy on the visitor's part could cause the bird to bite out of fear or excitement. Your bird, after all, does not know this person. Before this session, educate your visitor on the difference between biting and using the beak to "taste" the new finger or arm or for balance as your Quaker climbs aboard.

Other situations that might cause your bird to bite include sudden loud noises and some bright colors. Although a certain level of noise is preferable to birds, simulating the level that might be reached in the wild, startling sounds can indicate trouble and frighten a bird. For pet birds, such noises, as well as fast movements, cause an instinctive fight-or-flight reaction. Part of that natural, instinctive response could be a strong bite.

SCREAMING MIMIS

Screaming birds are unhappy birds. Owners of screaming birds are unhappy, too. A parrot's screams can shatter any semblance of peace in your home. Some screaming is to be expected, and the normal screaming of a parrot at dawn or dusk can take on a loudly joyful quality.

The screams of an unhappy parrot will make all in earshot wish they could do something about it. Reducing screaming requires some detective work on your part. First, of course, you must find out why your bird screams; this means watching her carefully to note when she does and does not scream. She may scream for a variety of reasons; many will involve the presence—or lack—of things she needs: food, your company, new or different toys, water to bathe in. The causes of screaming will differ somewhat from bird to bird.

Establishing a routine with your bird should help quell any screaming spells.

You can see the variety of things that brings on the behavior. Altering the behavior takes cleverness, not brute force, acrimonious reprisals or loud reprimands. Not only will these methods not work, they will make the screaming worse. Your bird will either seek the negative attention you are offering or continue in her confusion to seek what she wants in the only way she can: by screaming.

SET A SCHEDULE

Establish times during the day when you will feed your bird everything from seeds and pellets to fruits and vegetables, as well as snacks. Set up a time every day when you will offer her fresh water to drink and use for bathing. Imagine if you were dependent on someone to give you food, water, attention, anything you need to be happy. Wouldn't you be happy if it were scheduled to arrive at a set time each day and did so no matter what else was going on? The late arrival of food or water will make your bird scream in unhappiness, and rightly so. If your bird, like mine, wants to go to bed at the same time each day, give in to this need for a secure environment.

On the other hand, your bird will want to be with you and other members of your family constantly. If you have established the idea that you will hold and cuddle your bird, carrying her around with you all day, the first time you fail to do this, she will express her indignation by screaming. If you have led your bird to expect more of your time than you can give every day, you must help her make the adjustment to a more realistic expectation.

Quaker parrots live in large, gregarious flocks. They interact constantly during daylight hours. They live in close-knit communal nests. This is not a solitary or independent bird, whether wild or a pet. If your personality and lifestyle demand a more self-reliant bird, look elsewhere; a Quaker parrot is not that kind of bird.

chapter 6

Feeding
Your
Quaker Parrot

One way to determine what to feed a bird is to observe the eating habits of wild birds of a particular species. This is a good start, but by no means a perfect solution to the problem. Wild birds fly away when approached, leaving the observer to guess what they've eaten. Perhaps more important, it would be impossible to keep a flock of wild birds in sight for any extended  period of time, and who knows what they might eat while out of sight. In years of plenty, wild birds eat well, but in years when rainfall is low, they can eat only what is available. Our goal must be to match the best of possible diets to which wild birds might have access, and to choose the foods that would be available to them.

71

The Quaker Parrot's Diet

IN THE WILD

Wild Quaker parrots have been observed eating a variety of seeds, fruit, blossoms, insects, leaf buds, thistles, grasses and parts of trees—a varied diet. Near populated areas, the birds have also been known to eat sweet potatoes, legumes, drying meat, cereal crops, such as maize and sorghum, as well as citrus crops.

We understand that humans need a variety of foods to take in proper amounts of protein, calcium, carbohydrates and fats, and minerals and vitamins to maintain our bodily growth and energy requirements. The same is true of birds. Because no one food supplies all of the nutrients for good health, an assortment must be offered. In this way, a bird will be more likely to eat enough of the various nutrients she needs to maintain a long, healthy life.

All bird owners must dedicate themselves to offering their pets the best diet possible. Wild Quakers can live as long as thirty-five to forty years. Unfortunately, pet parrots do not have this luxury: Many die before they are five years old because of poor diet and lack of proper veterinary care.

SEEDS

Wild Quaker parrots eat an assortment of seeds, which indicates to me that we should offer our Quakers a good quality seed mix along with many other foods.

A seed mix would contain sunflower seeds, both black and striped; safflower seeds and smaller seeds. You should also offer millet. Quakers love millet sprays. Seeds should not, however, comprise the total diet. Again, keep in mind the variety of foods a wild bird eats.

TESTING SEEDS FOR FRESHNESS

It's critical to use fresh seed because it contains the most nutrients. You can easily find out if seed is fresh by trying to sprout it. Cut a piece of a new sponge. Put it in a small bowl of water until it has absorbed the water. Place the wet sponge on a small plate in the sun and sprinkle some seeds on the top, working them into the holes of the sponge. If you keep the sponge damp, fresh seeds will sprout. Do not feed these test seeds to your Quaker because you have not controlled the possible growth of bacteria or mold.

FRUITS AND VEGETABLES

Seeds, of course, do not a balanced diet make; fruits and vegetables are a necessary addition. The only members of this group you should not offer your bird are avocado and rhubarb leaves. Rhubarb leaves are poisonous to any animal, including humans. Otherwise, pick and choose among fruits and vegetables; this can be great fun.

Like wild Quaker parrots, your pet Quaker needs a varied diet.

Some of my birds' favorite fruits include pears, plums, apricots, apples, figs, passion fruit, strawberries, blackberries, raspberries, pomegranates, bananas, cherries and grapes. (Remove cherry pits and apple seeds, both of which could cause illness. As a general rule of thumb, remove seeds and pits from most fruits because they may be toxic. Exceptions are those that have tiny seeds like raspberries, grapes, strawberries, boysenberries and kiwi fruit.) All of my birds enjoy cooked plantains, now widely available.

The vegetables most popular among my flock are Brussels sprouts, red or green jalapeño peppers, red or green bell pepper with seeds, Chinese pea pods, English pea pods, broccoli, chicory, dandelion (purchased at the grocery store to avoid any pesticides and fertilizers to which wild dandelions may have been exposed), corn on the cob, carrots, beet greens, chickweed, spinach, tomatillos, sour cucumber, parsley and

73

chicory. Avoid eggplant, iceberg lettuce and any other pale lettuce; they offer little or no nutritional value, outside of water and fiber.

Dried Fruits

If you have a season when fresh fruits are unavailable at reasonable prices, you can offer dried fruits. To make them more appealing, soak them. Discard them on the same schedule you use for fresh or cooked food.

Experimenting with different fruits and vegetables is a fun way to keep your bird healthy.

Quaker parrots relish leafy vegetables. One way to make them a special treat is to rinse veggie leaves in cold water just prior to hanging them in the cage. Right on the top of your Quaker's hit list are eating, playing and bathing in water, making this combination a triple treat. Your delighted bird may rub against the wet leaves to take a bath, perhaps nibbling as he does so.

THE IMPORTANCE OF CLEAN FOOD

Most fresh food will be contaminated as it grows and while it is stored near the fields or even in warehouses that service local markets or grocery chains. This includes organically grown fruits and vegetables, which should be free of pesticides, but not necessarily free of other contaminants.

Scrubbing the skin of such food with liquid dish soap and water will suffice in most instances. You must be sure to rinse the food well to remove any soap, dirt or bacteria. Dry with paper towels and store as usual in your refrigerator. This treatment will be enough for most healthy, unstressed birds.

If your birds become ill, ask your vet about a product called Nolvasan. This nontoxic liquid is used to clean surfaces in veterinary hospitals and does not require rinsing. You can order it through your vet. Ask for instructions for use on vegetables and fruits.

When to Discard Food

Depending on the temperature in the house, I discard the food either four (in summer) or eight (in winter) hours after feeding it to my birds. If you work outside of your home, feed a seed and pellet mixture in the morning and the fresh food in the evening when you return home. Maintain your schedule on the weekends so your bird always knows what to expect.

If it begins to smell too fruity or ripe in your home, throw away the food. There will be waste and plenty of it. Wild birds eat only part of each thing they try, and your bird's habits will be the same. It will not be economical to try to recycle this food and give it to your bird again; spoiled food can make your bird ill, and a visit to the vet can be traumatic and expensive.

People Food

Quaker parrots need protein and calcium for good health. Although they can get some from fruits and vegetables, most notably broccoli, it's best to offer other good sources such as cheese and egg. My birds enjoy cheddar cheese, jack cheese, scrambled or boiled egg, steak, hamburger, pork and pork bones and chicken and chicken bones. All egg and meat should be well-cooked to kill any bacteria that may contaminate the food. Offer cheese only in small portions. My birds also

---

SPROUTING FRESH SEED

The most nutritious seeds are sprouted. This process is easy, but must be done carefully. The best candidates are millet, wheat, oat and sunflower seeds. Place a tablespoonful of seeds in a bowl. Cover them with tepid water. Put a loose lid on the bowl and leave the seeds for about twelve hours in a warm home, or twenty-four hours in a cold home. Rinse the seeds well, looking carefully for any that are oozing a liquid or look as if they may have fungi or mold growing on them. You can sprout dried beans such as garbanzo and mung, as well as adzuki peas and whole green peas. Wheat berries also grow into delicious, healthful sprouts. If many in the batch are spoiled, throw them all out. Dry the seeds between multiple layers of paper towels, and then feed them to your birds. To avoid the possibility of digestive upsets due to spoiled food, throw away any seeds left uneaten after four hours.

demand baked (or microwaved) sweet potatoes, squash, pasta and cooked rice. I often cook a batch of kidney beans, split peas, pinto beans or pink beans and brown rice for my birds. Some birdkeepers cook a mixture of dried beans to feed their birds once a day.

I use the microwave to reheat all frozen food. I recommend this with a note of caution: After the food has been cooked in a microwave, mix it well and cool thoroughly. Microwave cooking creates hot spots you might not be aware of, but that could burn your bird's crop if he gulps the hot food.

GRAINS

Grains also offer good nutrition to your birds. I suggest you add hulled millet, quinoa, wheat berries, bulgar wheat, buckwheat groats, pearled barley and tritcale to your bird's diet. Cook either a single kind or mixtures of these and freeze in portions of about 2 tablespoons—an average serving size. Reheat in the microwave, stir well and serve to your feathered gourmand. Do not add salt or sugar to the grains.

In short, my birds eat what we eat, with the exception of avocado, alcohol, chocolate and large portions of dairy products. Birds do not have the enzyme necessary to digest dairy products. Chocolate (theobromine, a chemical component of chocolate) is poisonous to most animals, including birds.

In addition to their seeds, grains and fresh fruits and veggies, your Quaker may eat cooked oatmeal, French toast, pancakes or eggs for breakfast. For lunch, whatever sandwich or cheese and crackers we eat can make a fine Quaker meal.

Formulated, or Pelleted, Food

Nutrition is a major concern with all of us, but it is of particular concern to avian veterinarians. This is because, despite a much longer expected life span in the wild, the average pet bird lives only about five years. The cause of death is often malnutrition. To help alleviate this problem, many bird food companies and veterinarians have worked on formulating pellets to meet the nutritional needs of various species of birds. Check with your avian veterinarian on types and qualities available.

To help ensure good overall nutrition and prevent boredom, I do not offer pelleted food alone, nor do I recommend it as a sole source of nutrition. I offer pelleted food each day in addition to seeds, fruits and vegetables and cooked foods. My reasoning is that wild birds eat a huge assortment of foods, which helps them to obtain all of the nutrition that they need. Aside from nutritional consideration, I want to allay boredom. Perhaps most importantly, to date only one parrot has been studied thoroughly enough to have a pelleted food formulated that matches its nutritional needs exactly. That parrot is the cockatiel.

If you decide to add pelleted food to your bird's diet, use only one kind. These foods have been carefully formulated to include vitamins and minerals. Never offer additional vitamins to your bird's food if you are already offering vitamin-fortified pellets or seeds. Mixing types can off-set the planned balance or overdose your bird.

Providing good nutrition will help your Quaker live a longer and healthier life.

Watching birds eat can be great fun. They rip into food, throw it, wipe it all over cage bars and perches, stand on it and feed it to each other (and will offer it to you, too). For a bird, food is fun. However, birds are no better than most humans at choosing to eat a balanced diet of what is best for them. I offer a wide variety of foods in homemade mixes we call salads, as well as their seeds, pellets and cooked food. I do this and hope that what they eat of each will help them ingest a balanced diet. My birds are rarely sick and none show signs of slowing down, although all passed the dreaded five-year mark long ago. I expect that they will all live to ripe old ages. Why? Good nutrition, in addition to proper medical care from an avian vet.

When and How to Feed Your Bird

Make fresh, healthful food available to your bird all day and into the evening. Whoever coined the phrase "to eat like a bird" obviously had no idea how birds really eat. Birds metabolize food quickly, but their digestive systems are small, which means a bird cannot eat much at one time, but will need to eat many times a day. The amount of food one healthy Quaker parrot

A healthy, active Quaker will have a great appetite.

consumes during the day will surely surprise you. They love to eat, and because they are so active, they need to eat often.

MAINTAIN A ROUTINE

Develop a regular schedule for feeding your bird. He is completely dependent on you for food and will feel more secure if he knows when he will eat each day. An added benefit is that you will be sure to feed your bird and will remove food before it spoils.

If you find that you are rushing in the morning, fix the fruits and veggies at night; keep them in the refrigerator until the next morning, when you feed them to your bird. You can give the bird the fresh seed and water just before you put him to bed. If the perches are placed correctly in the cage, food should remain unsoiled throughout the night. Share some of your breakfast and dinner food with your bird, including fruit, vegetables, cooked grains and cereal and meat. If you are home for lunch, you can share that, too.

Offer New Food Regularly

When you offer your bird new foods, he may at first reject them. This is normal, and probably based on an instinct to avoid unknown, possibly poisonous, foods. Hand-fed birds usually adapt to new foods with greater ease than parent-fed or feral birds. Nevertheless, with either kind of bird, continue to offer the new food. Your bird may reject it for six months or several years. In the end, he will eventually try it, and may find a new favorite. My birds are especially prone to try new foods when they can see us eat the foods, too.

Monitor Intake

Keep a written record of what your bird eats. This record will help you in a dramatically important way: A poor appetite may be the first sign of illness. If you know with certainty what and how much your bird eats each day, you will notice immediately when his habits change; this can be critical to your bird's health.

Keep track of how much your bird is eating—a poor appetite is one of the first signs of illness.

Vitamins

A lot of what makes nutritional sense for humans makes sense for birds. If your bird eats a varied, balanced diet, he does not need supplemental vitamins. If you think your bird needs them, check with your avian veterinarian. Never assume that your bird needs more of one kind of vitamin or mineral than another. An overdose of some vitamins can endanger your bird's health or kill him.

Never put vitamin drops in your bird's drinking water. The drops can make the water unpalatable and may

spoil before you change the water. In all my years of
birdkeeping, I have never given my birds supplemental
vitamins. The dangers from overdosing on various vitamins are many and easily avoided.

Things to Avoid

In the past, aviculturists and veterinarians often rec-
ommended that we offer our birds cuttlebone and grit.
In Europe and Australia, many birdkeepers continue
this practice. In North America, however, these items
are not considered a good food choice.

*A well-balanced
diet will help keep
your Quaker free
of respiratory infec-
tions, poor feather
condition, flaky
skin and reproduc-
tive problems.*

Do not pick wild grass seeds, leaf buds and branches
for your bird. These items could have been sprayed
with insecticides or herbicides, both of which are toxic.
If you garden organically, you can feed your birds food
from your garden. If you use any kind of pesticide or
systemic fertilizer, do not feed food from your garden
to your bird.

chapter 7

Preventive
Care for Your
Quaker Parrot

Daily Concerns

Eliminating potential hazards and maintaining healthful conditions in your home and your Quaker parrot's cage will prevent most health problems. Before you buy your bird, take care of as many foreseeable problems as possible.

HOUSEHOLD HAZARDS

Quaker parrots chew constantly and they are not discriminating. This behavior can probably be related to their extraordinary nest-building habits. Unless you have cleared your home of hazards, your bird could quickly find herself in danger, or too sick or injured to revive. Put all wires out of sight, including electrical cords and those leading to your phones and antennas. The squish of the plastic covering on cords seems to be irresistible to Quaker parrots. To protect your bird, place the cords in ½- to 1-inch-diameter PVC piping. Run this piping around the baseboards in the room from any appliances to their electrical outlet. If you smoke, do not do so in the house. The smoke will definitely shorten your bird's life. Keep all cigarettes and cigarette butts out of the house. Your Quaker will find them irresistible for tasting and may quickly become ill or die.

Ceiling fans are just one of the household hazards you must watch out for when your bird is out of her cage.

Some household dangers cannot be removed, but must be monitored to prevent injury to your new pet. These hazards include rotating ceiling fans, aquariums without hoods, open toilets, knickknacks and radiant heaters. Even though your Quaker will have her wings clipped, you can assume nothing; it's your job to make the room as safe as possible. A frightened or startled bird can fly surprisingly far. A bird with a few wing feathers grown in unnoticed by you can also fly far enough to get hurt or escape.

Before your bird comes out of her cage, shut all windows and doors, and restrain other pets. Try to think ahead of any lurking danger.

Remove from your home any poisonous plants. Pet Quaker parrots cannot differentiate between safe and unsafe plants. Never allow your bird to nibble on flower arrangements.

Close all doors and windows before your Quaker has the freedom of the house.

The Poison Hotline

The list in the "Plant Precautions" sidebar is by no means complete. If your bird eats something that you suspect may be poisonous, call your vet or the ASPCA hotline for help. The ASPCA hotline number is (800) 548-2423. They will charge you $30 for the consultation.

Look Out for Lead

Lead is another potential hazard. Do not allow your bird to chew any painted surface. Paint, particularly older paint, often contains lead. Other things contain lead, too, including costume jewelry, eyeglass frames and the seams between panes in stained-glass windows or art objects. Old or collectible toys, such as soldiers, may contain lead. Other objects to beware of include belt buckles and chain-link–style belts, Christmas ornaments, pewter figurines, souvenir

> ### PLANT PRECAUTIONS
>
> Common toxic plants: ivy, azaleas, elephant ear, euphorbia, potato sprouts and leaves, creeping Charlie, aloe, philodendron and asparagus fern.
>
> Poisonous flowering plants: snapdragons, hyacinth, hydrangea, daffodils, chrysanthemums, geraniums, holly, oleander, sweet peas, amaryllis, bluebonnets, calla lilies, crocuses, larkspurs, impatiens, jasmine, lantanas, lilies of the valley, mock oranges, morning glories, narcissus, peonies, pinks, poppies, some rosemary and sage and tulips.

spoons, lamp finials, key-chain ornaments, metal bookends and picture frames, Linotype and lead-foil seals on wine bottles (newer bottles of wine use a plastic seal).

Remember to keep your birds away from any plants that may be poisonous.

Unbelievably, some bird toys may also contain lead. Of particular concern in the past have been the little weighted toys that birds love to knock down and watch bounce back; the bottoms of these toys often contain lead weights. Curtain weights also may be made of lead. If in doubt, keep it away from your bird. If you need curtain weights, for example, use something edible or nontoxic. If you have children in your home, this could serve as a wake-up call; lead is dangerous to children, too. Zinc is also said to be toxic to birds. Some wire cages made for rabbits or other small mammals are unsuitable for birds. The type of metal they are made of may contain zinc or other potentially toxic metals.

ABOUT TEFLON

Another dangerous item is Teflon. At high heat—about 536° Fahrenheit—Teflon emits a gas that can kill your bird. Because birds are far more sensitive to this gas than humans or other animals, you may not know that the gas is present until the bird becomes ill or dies.

I removed all Teflon-coated pans from my home to prevent an accident. Although I am sure I won't overheat these pans, visitors to my home, as well as other family members, are not as acutely aware of the problem as I am. Even if you take the same precaution, you may have normal household items that have Teflon coating. Some hair dryers and space heaters have

Teflon-coated parts. When these items are heated, as they are meant to be, the Teflon may emit toxic fumes—perhaps enough to kill your bird. The old adage, better safe than sorry, is a good one to follow.

STRONG SCENTS

Another potential danger is anything with a scent. Do not spray perfume or cologne when your bird is visiting the room. Avoid burning scented wood in the fireplace. There have been some claims of scented candles killing birds. I have seen no substantiation of this, but I tend to err on the side of caution. Fumes from paint, cleaning supplies and pesticides are also dangerous and may kill your bird. Do not hang freshly dry-cleaned clothing or draperies in the same room your bird is in.

THE LEG BAND

Another common danger is the leg band. Many domestically bred birds will have a leg band to identify the breeder and perhaps the date of birth. I recommend that you ask your vet to take this band off your bird's leg. Keep it in a safe place if you plan to breed or show the bird, or if your state requires it. I feel strongly about this because of the number of birds that catch this band on hooks, cloth, string or parts of their cages. If left undiscovered, the bird could lose her leg or her life.

Other Pets and Children

You can have other pets if you have birds, but certain precautions must be taken. Mammal saliva can be toxic to birds if it enters a wound or if the bird ingests it orally. Cats that live with birds should be declawed.

TEACHING KIDS TO BE CAREFUL

My two-and-a-half-year-old grandson spends every day with us during the week. Although we tried mightily, we could not seem to impress on him the danger of a parrot's bite—until one of our more temperamental birds bit my husband, causing a large, bleeding wound. Nicky saw this happen and talked endlessly about the situation. He now stays away from all parrots unless we take part in the interaction. Do I trust Nicky to stay away all the time? No. I still keep a close eye on the situation, for his safety and for that of my birds.

85

Both cats and dogs can be taught to respect and stay away from birds.

Some people, in order to teach their cat or dog to be wary, allow their birds to bite the noses of cats or dogs under controlled conditions. This works well with young cats and dogs. Of course, the cat or dog must be restrained during the lesson. Still, *never* leave a bird and a cat or dog together unattended.

It is generally not a good idea to allow Quaker parrots access to birds of other species, especially smaller birds. Although feral Quakers are known for allowing other animals and bird species to live in abandoned parts of their nests, pet Quakers are tremendously territorial and may injure or kill the other birds.

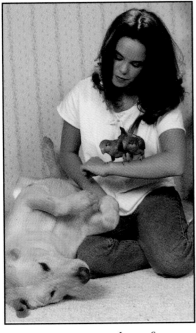

Closely supervise any interaction your Quaker has with other pets.

Children can also be a danger. They move quickly and are often unaware of how fragile a bird can be. If a bird bites a child, the child's natural reaction may be fatal to the bird. After children are about four or five years old, you can teach them how to handle a bird safely, but you must still supervise for several more years, depending on the maturity of the child and the bird's personality.

Regular Care

The importance of routine care cannot be stressed enough. Once you have established a daily routine, it will take very little time, but will ensure your bird's health and happiness.

CAGE CLEANING

Every day—without fail—you should clean the bottom of your bird's cage, changing the cage floor covering. Hot soap and water will help kill most bacteria. If you feel the need for a stronger cleaner, you can use a 10 percent bleach/90 percent water solution. Rinse anything dipped in this solution thoroughly before returning it to the bird's cage.

Every day, change all dishes for clean ones filled with fresh clean seed, water and soft food. A few hours after you put cooked food in the cage, remove it. In warm weather or an overheated home, do not leave uneaten food in the cage for more than an hour. If you would not eat it, do not offer it to your bird.

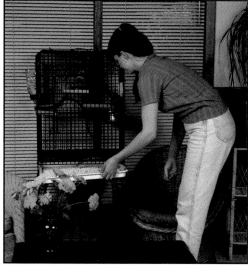

When you clean the cage, look at the bird's droppings. Are they the same color as usual? Are they firm and round, with green on the outside and white on the inside of the droppings? Are there about as many as usual? Did the bird eat well—about as much as she usually does? This inspection will soon become second nature to you, but is often the first clue to the state of your bird's health.

Be sure to clean the bottom of your Quaker's cage and change the cage floor covering every day.

At least monthly, you should scrub the whole cage to remove any droppings and old food from the perches, sides and floor. Use hot water and detergent. If you have the time, do this job once a week. In the end, the weekly cleaning takes much less time than it would if you had waited a month.

GROOMING

In the wild, healthy birds are well-groomed. Keeping your pet bird well-groomed is easy. A healthy bird's beak shouldn't need trimming. If your bird's beak suddenly begins to overgrow, take her to your vet immediately. This could be a sign of ill health. Do not try to trim a bird's beak yourself. You could do serious damage to this important body part.

If you have provided a variety of perches in different shapes and widths, your Quaker parrot's toenails should wear to the proper length naturally. If the bird's nails grow too long, though, they could become a danger—catching in cloth and tearing into the vein, which could bleed excessively. Talk to your vet about the proper length and how to clip them if necessary.

Bathing

Grooming is an essential part of a healthy Quaker's daily routine, both in the wild and in your home. Bathing will remove any dirt or food from your bird's feathers and will encourage your bird to preen her feathers, an essential grooming technique that birds must perform many times daily to keep their feathers in top condition. It has also been proven in several species, including Quaker parrots, that daily bathing, especially where there is low humidity, can help prevent birds from beginning to pull, or pluck, their own feathers.

Quaker parrots love water—a simple spray or small bathing bowl will do.

Bathing a Quaker is usually simple; they love water and most will bathe willingly in a shallow, wide-mouthed bowl placed on the bottom of the cage. Most will also love frolicking in the spray of a misting bottle or in a shower with you. You can either buy or make a perch of PVC pipe that will adhere to the shower stall wall.

Recovering a Lost Bird

All pet Quaker parrots should have their wings clipped. There should be no exception to this rule. This will help them behave as polite members of your family, and it will help prevent them from escaping. Wing clipping is a process that must be repeated over and over, as soon as new feathers grow in. However, if your bird is frightened near an open door or window, he may fly away even with clipped wings.

While it's difficult to recover a lost bird, it's not impossible. Perhaps because Quaker parrots are so social, many escaped pets fly to other people, whom they may hope will help them. This makes Quaker parrots especially good subjects for a new innovation: microchips. It's now possible to have an encoded microchip placed under your bird's skin. If the bird is captured by someone else, her chip can be read to determine who the owners are. An avian veterinarian can implant the chip. Some avian vets and SPCAs have now bought the equipment to read the microchips, which would identify your bird beyond doubt. You could also have your bird tattooed or her DNA prints recorded for later identification.

If your bird is lost, try setting up her cage outside, away from people and stocked with lots of food and treats.

If your bird has flown away, advertise in newspapers, and put up posters in pet stores and veterinarians' offices. Many communities have networks that shelter lost pets and will help owners to look for them. Local on-line service providers may provide bulletin boards for lost pets, and any animal shelters in your area should be notified.

Other methods for recovering a lost bird include taping your bird's calls ahead of time and replaying the tape loudly outside to attract the bird back to you or to her cage, which you should place away from people, fully stocked with food and treats. The best solution, though, is prevention.

Make sure all windows and doors are closed before your bird comes out of her cage. Do not allow your bird to ride on your shoulder. Besides behavioral problems, it is far too easy to forget the bird and walk outside. The mere shock of being outside may cause your bird to fly away in fright.

Traveling with Your Bird

When you travel with your bird in the car, always carry her in a closed container. It's tempting to let a bird run around in the car; however, if you are involved in a traffic accident or if you absentmindedly open a window, your bird could be lost. Your mischievous Quaker might also take the opportunity to bite your ear or face while you are driving, especially if she is sitting on your shoulder or the back of the seat. Many styles of travel container are on the market, some from mail-order catalogs or bird-magazine advertisements.

The ideal travel container can be used in a car, a plane or a train. It should have at least one perch and food and water dishes. If you are traveling a great distance, you may find it more convenient to offer fruit and vegetables in place of water, which spills easily. Attach the carrier to the seat with a seat belt, and keep the bird inside her carrier while you are traveling.

Avoid overheating or cooling the bird. This includes keeping the bird away from direct sunlight and heating and air-conditioning vents. If you plan to travel by plane, make reservations ahead so you can take your bird inside the plane's cabin. Often, only one pet is allowed inside each part of the cabin: economy, business and first class.

All of my birds' travel cages and car carriers have sturdy locks and a label with my name, phone number and address. If I am in an accident and have lost consciousness, the label will identify who owned the birds—and who I am.

Your
Quaker Parrot's
Health

Choosing a veterinarian is one of the most important tasks you will undertake for your bird. The vet must be a qualified avian veterinarian. How do you find one?

Choosing a Veterinarian

If you have joined or visited a parrot or Quaker parrot club, members will have recommendations. The pet store or breeder from whom you buy the bird may also be able to advise you; however, I would not be comfortable taking a new bird to a veterinar-

ian associated with the breeder or pet store where I bought the bird. If these methods fail, you can call any veterinarian and ask who in the area is qualified to treat birds.

Most areas have wild-bird rehabilitators who are happy to advise you on who in your area is the best avian vet. I used this latter method to find an avian veterinarian when I made my last move. Out of curiosity, I also asked the veterinarian who treats my dog to recommend an avian veterinarian. She gave me the same name as had the wild-bird rehabilitator.

What You Should Ask

On your first visit, ask plenty of questions. Some you might include are "Do you take continuing education courses in avian veterinary medicine?" "Are you a certified avian veterinarian?" "How many birds do you see each week?" "Are lab tests done in-house or sent out?" "Who sees my bird if he is injured or becomes ill on a weekend or after hours?" If you are not satisfied with the answers, continue looking. Don't wait until your bird is ill.

Signs of Illness

In the wild, an animal that is weakened by injury or illness is the first one a predator will choose to attack. From the predator's point of view, it makes good sense. This animal will be easier to catch than a healthy member of the group. Probably for this reason, birds instinctively hide signs of illness. It's not a conscious decision; some survival behaviors, including this one, occur spontaneously. It's not impossible, though, for an alert owner to spot signs of illness long before anyone else can.

I got up one morning and noticed a slightly dazed look in my normally rambunctious bird's eyes. Doodle is usually alert and full of attitude. I made a vet appointment immediately and took Doodle's mate, too. I reasoned that if Doodle were ill, Yankee would be soon. They fed each other, bathed in the same bowl, ate the same food and slept nestled close together.

At first glance, my vet, who is an experienced avian veterinarian, was mystified by my assertion that Doodle was ill. To him, she looked fine. Lab tests, though, revealed an infection. Because we caught it in time, Doodle recovered quickly and has been healthy ever since.

KNOW YOUR BIRD

The way to spot illness before it becomes obvious is to know exactly how your bird looks and acts when he is well. Quaker parrots are active birds, constantly looking for mischief. If the level of activity is slower than normal, look for other signs of illness: Take the whole bird into consideration. Activity is just one sign. Look for reasons he might be slower than normal. Is it much colder in the house than usual? Hotter? Do you have visitors? Are there any other changes in the bird's physical surroundings, such as balloons brought in for a party or a new light fixture? Birds are wary of altered environments and will watch cautiously to be sure the modification doesn't mean danger. In the face of danger, they do not want to draw attention to themselves.

Since birds tend to hide illness, you should note how your Quaker looks and acts when he is well.

CHECK THE CAGE BOTTOM

Each day, as you change the covering on the bottom of your bird's cage, notice what his droppings look like. They should be firm and round, green on the outside and white on the inside. Loose yellowish or bright-green droppings, for instance, are not normal. All-white droppings indicate trouble, too, as do those that are red or blackish. Again, though, look at the whole picture before jumping to a conclusion.

93

If the bird has eaten lots of fruits or vegetables of those colors, his droppings will reflect this. So, if your bird's droppings are tinged with red, but he is active, his eyes are bright and clear and he has eaten beets, strawberries or other red food, the food is probably the cause of the unusual droppings. Watch for a return to normal-colored droppings.

DO A DAILY HEALTH CHECK

Keep track of your Quaker's normal routine so you will know by his behavior if something's wrong.

Look carefully at your new Quaker parrot several times each day to become familiar with what he looks like at various times of the day. Make a mental note of the time he normally awakens. When is he active or inactive during the day? Most birds wake up early in the morning and are active until afternoon, when they take naps. They awaken again in time for the family dinner and will remain active until bedtime. If you work swing shift or a nighttime shift, your bird may adjust his schedule to suit your active times. Always be sure, though, that your bird gets about ten to twelve hours of sleep at night.

INTAKE AND OUTPUT

Each time you remove your bird's seed, water and fresh food, take a good look at what he has eaten and how much he drank. Also check to see if he has fouled his drinking water or any food with droppings or old food. If there are droppings in the water or food, move some perches or relocate the dish away from perches. If there is food in the water, relocate those dishes away from the fresh food dish.

How much of each does your pet eat daily? Make a mental note. The amount eaten each day is another good indicator of your bird's general health and well-being. The first few days at home, your bird may not eat much. He will need a few days to adjust to your home. Base your assessment of what he should eat on days after he has adjusted to living with you.

Your Quaker's food and water intake is a good indicator of his health status.

How to Detect Illness

In general, if your bird is inactive and sleeping much more than is normal, if he is eating less, if his droppings are loose or discolored, if his eyes are dull and if he sits listlessly on his perch with feathers fluffed, he is sick. If he sits on the bottom of his cage instead of on his perch, he is probably desperately ill. Healthy birds perch as high as they can. Instinctively, birds seem to know that sitting high up helps to keep them away from danger. Well birds sleep balanced on one foot. Sick birds tend to sleep on two feet.

Other signs of illness include discharge from a bird's nose or beak or both. If the beak begins to grow at an odd angle or suddenly begins to overgrow and appears to need trimming, your bird may have

> ## SIGNS OF POSSIBLE ILLNESS
>
> Nasal discharge
>
> Swollen, tired, dull or runny eyes
>
> Labored breathing, wheezing
>
> Sleeping on two feet all the time
>
> Resting for long periods of time on the cage bottom
>
> Weight loss
>
> Oddly shaped feathers
>
> Excessive scratching, leading to bald patches
>
> Lumps on his body
>
> Swollen leg scales
>
> Inactivity and fluffed feathers
>
> Discolored droppings
>
> Screaming as the bird pulls his feathers

become ill. Also look closely for other signs such as labored breathing, wheezing or productive sneezing (in which a discharge comes out of the bird's nasal

95

A healthy bird's nose, beak and eyes are free of discharge.

passage). Feather problems can also signal illness. An abundance of clubbed, frayed, chewed or oddly shaped feathers, bald patches on the bird's body and excessive scratching and screaming as the bird yanks out feathers all indicate the need to see a veterinarian.

What to Do

If your bird appears to be ill, call your veterinarian for an appointment immediately. Don't try to diagnose the illness yourself. Birds are complex animals; it is difficult even for an experienced avian veterinarian to determine what is wrong and which treatment methods will be most effective.

Proper Use of Medications

If your avian vet prescribes an antibiotic, be sure to administer it exactly as ordered. This includes using all of the medication. If you stop early, you may give the bacteria that caused the infection a chance to become immune to the medication.

About OTC Medications

Many over-the-counter medications are available in retail stores. Do not offer them to your bird unless you have been directed to do so by a veterinarian. These preparations could mask the signs of a bird's illness, making it more difficult to diagnose as the bird becomes progressively more ill. Offering these drugs to your bird could kill the beneficial bacteria in your bird's gut, allowing harmful bacteria to grow unchecked. Such drugs might also aggravate the bird's condition, making him sicker than he was before you medicated him.

Parasites

Despite what you may read in many other parrot-care books, especially those written for European or

Australian keepers, parasites in pet parrots are uncommon. Never use insecticides in your bird's cage or nest box; nor should you ever use them *on* your bird.

I strongly recommend against birdkeepers' trying to diagnose *any* health problem—including parasites. If your bird is thin or losing weight despite a hearty appetite, or if he shows some unusual beak growth or odd-looking scales on his legs, take him to your vet for an accurate diagnosis. Never install a mite protector in your bird's cage. These are not only ineffective, they are dangerous to your bird's health.

Administer all prescribed medication to your bird exactly as it is ordered by the veterinarian.

Prevention Is the Best Cure

A Quaker parrot that eats a nutritious, well-balanced diet and is kept in clean surroundings is a hardy pet. Keeping your Quaker parrot's food healthful will not be difficult, but may require you to change some habits. The effort that goes into taking good care of a Quaker parrot, though, will result in a more healthful environment for all of the inhabitants, including you!

Cleanliness Counts

Keep everything clean, paying special attention to the food preparation areas of your kitchen, from the counters and utensils to the sinks. Of course, there is the obvious: If you handle raw beef, pork or chicken, you must use an antibacterial cleaner on anything the meat might have touched, including your hands. Make careful hand washing a habit before and after handling any food.

Never use a wooden chopping block to cut up fruits and vegetables if you have also used it to cut meat. For bird food, I always use the same cutting board—one made of plastic. Each time I use it, I wash it in the dishwasher. Also wash sponges in the dishwasher or soak them in a 10 percent bleach/90 percent water solution, and use only paper towels to dry counters and utensils; cloth dish- and washcloths can harbor bacteria, even if freshly laundered. Do not offer your bird any food you have had in your mouth—don't even bite off a piece and then give it to your bird.

Health Hazards

AIRBORNE TOXINS

Birds have sensitive lungs, and many things we use around the house as a matter of course can be toxic to them.

Nonstick coatings on pots and pans, hair dryers and space heaters can emit fumes that will kill birds if overheated—about 536° Fahrenheit. While this implies misuse of the equipment, it occurs often enough that I gave away all of my nonstick pans, as well as blow dryers and space heaters that have wires covered in Teflon. If in doubt, call the manufacturer for information on the inclusion of Teflon in the product.

Other sources of toxic fumes include paint, perfumes and other scented items, as well as most insecticides. Many of us have our homes sprayed for insects. Before you do so, ask the company to certify that the chemicals it uses are nontoxic to birds. Any spray with a potential for harming human children will certainly be toxic to birds.

Other problem substances include most things that come in spray bottles, such as clothes starch, cooking oil, hair spray, pesticides, herbicides, oven cleaner, house paint, spot remover, deodorants, perfume,

shellac, sun-tan lotions and flea bombs. Often the pro-
pellant is as dangerous as the contents of the can.

HUMANS CAN BE A HEALTH HAZARD, TOO

As much as you love your bird, you could still be hazardous to his health. A few precautions will remedy the
situation, though.

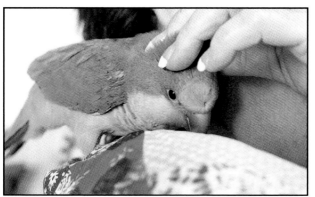

*It's okay to cud-
dle your Quaker,
but keep kisses to
a minimum.*

Your mouth is home to many bacteria harmful to your
bird. Do not allow your bird to touch your tongue or
teeth with his beak or tongue. Do not share food that
has been in your mouth. If you kiss your bird, plant the
kiss firmly on the front of his beak or on the top of his
head. This will keep your saliva away from the bird's
mouth. I do not kiss my birds' bodies; I don't want to
leave traces of bacteria they may pick up when they
preen their feathers.

When you visit pet stores, bird shows or a friend who
owns a bird, change clothes, shower and wash your
hair before you handle your bird. Many viruses and
bacteria can be carried on your skin, hair or clothing.
If your bird comes into contact with these viruses, he
could become ill. For this reason, I do not let people
whose birds may not be healthy handle my birds. Nor
do I take my birds to bird club meetings, for obvious
reasons.

HOUSEHOLD DANGER AREAS

The two most dangerous rooms in your home will
probably be the kitchen and the bathroom. Cooking

spray and other fumes, as well as the cooking process, present a major danger to your Quaker parrot. If these birds were not so curious and intelligent, they might not get into as much trouble in these rooms as they do. However, a little forewarning will help you prevent disaster. While you cook, lock your bird in her cage. Hot appliances, food, steam, constantly changing temperatures and fumes all combine to make the kitchen a hazardous place for birds.

*Prevent problems
by keeping your
Quaker locked in
his cage when
you are cooking.*

Bathrooms are equally dangerous because they are filled with toxic substances, such as deodorants, cleaning products, make up and perfumes. The most deadly part of the bathroom is standing water in toilets or sinks. Too many birds have needlessly drowned in bathrooms. If you take your bird in the bathroom to train or to accompany you on your rounds, take proper precautions before the visit.

Quarantine—What It Is and How to Do It

You should quarantine any new birds that you buy. Although standard practice cited by many birdkeepers is to quarantine a new bird for twenty-one days, it is better to keep him separate from your other birds for ninety days. Some bird diseases can take that long to develop.

Put the new bird in a separate room and never mingle the perches, toys or food and water dishes with those that belong to your other birds. Wash all food dishes in the dishwasher. Wash your hands carefully before handling your older birds, and always dry them on paper towels. When you first buy the new bird, have your avian vet give him a thorough check-up. Have one more set of blood tests and feces cultures run after ninety days.

First Aid

Regardless of how careful you are, your clever Quaker parrot may injure himself and require first aid to keep him stable until you can get him to a qualified veterinarian.

BLEEDING TOENAILS

Never allow your bird's toenails to overgrow. If they have become so sharp that they are uncomfortable on your finger or shoulder, it's time to trim them. Ask your vet to show you how to do this. Take your own towel to hold the bird. This ensures that the towel used has no harmful bacteria; items in veterinarian's offices can harbor bacteria and viruses from other birds' illnesses.

When you cut the toenails, keep styptic powder, cornstarch or flour nearby to press against the nail if you cut too deeply and bleeding begins. Press until the bleeding stops.

Allowing a bird's toenails to overgrow can be dangerous. Long, sharp toenails can catch on parts of the cage, in fabric around the house or on cloth or hemp perches. If a claw tears, the bird could bleed to death. In addition, the bird's claw could catch and panic the bird, causing him to chew off his leg. Prevention is simple: Keep the bird's nails trimmed.

TORN NAILS OR A BROKEN BEAK

If your bird tears a nail or breaks off the end of his beak and begins to bleed, you can stop the bleeding with styptic powder or, my favorites, flour or cornstarch. With your finger, press a pinch of cornstarch, flour or styptic powder against the wound for a minute or more. Pull your finger away. If blood begins to soak through the powder, put pressure on the wound until the bleeding stops. Next step? Call the veterinarian.

BLOOD FEATHERS

Blood feathers are another source of potential problems. As new feathers grow in, they are supplied with blood. When they finish growing, the blood supply is cut off. A blood feather is one that is still growing and has a blood supply. The base, or shaft, of the feather looks dark red, whereas other feathers have a semi-clear shaft. If a bird breaks a blood feather, blood will flow freely from the damaged shaft.

Styptic powder, tweezers, towels and gauze are good things to keep in your Quaker's first-aid kit.

To stop the blood flow, pull the blood feather out with a sturdy pair of tweezers or needle-nosed pliers. If you cannot do this or are unsure of how to do it, staunch the flow of blood with cornstarch and the pressure from your finger. Take the bird to your vet, who will show you how to pull the feather.

If you decide to clip your bird's wings regularly, you must avoid any blood feathers. Before I cut wing feathers, I locate blood feathers and then leave several feathers intact around the blood feather to protect it from the normal wear and tear that will be inflicted by the bird. After the blood has receded in the feather, I trim it and the feathers around it.

SIMPLE CUT OR LACERATION

A simple cut or laceration may bleed. To stop this, press a clean gauze pad against the wound until the bleeding stops. Do not put an antibiotic cream made for humans on the wound unless instructed to do so by your vet.

SHOCK

Shock is another condition requiring first aid. This can result from a bird's collision with anything solid, such as a wall, window or mirror. If you suspect shock, wrap the bird loosely in a towel for a few minutes, to keep him warm and still. If you and your bird have bonded closely, hold him to your chest so he can hear your heartbeat. In a minute or two, the bird should have recovered. If the effects linger, call your vet. Remember to keep the bird warm while you transport him to the vet's office.

EGG-BINDING

Egg-binding can cause significant problems. Your understanding of the condition and knowledge of how to treat it could save your bird's life. Of course, only female birds are afflicted with this problem, but because it is difficult to tell Quaker parrot males from females, you may unknowingly have a female bird. Unmated females can and will lay eggs; usually a healthy Quaker parrot will have no problems laying eggs.

An egg-bound female cannot pass her egg. This results not only in the retention of the egg, but in the prevention of her passing waste material. Signs of the condition include feather fluffing and sitting on the bottom of the cage looking miserable. Pick up the bird gently to visually examine her vent. If she appears to be swollen, suspect egg-binding. Handle her cautiously; breaking an egg inside a bird can result in a disastrous, perhaps fatal, infection.

First, wrap her in a towel to keep her warm. Unwrap the towel to reveal her vent, under her tail. Carefully apply petroleum jelly around her cloaca and return her to the towel. Call your veterinarian immediately.

OTHER ANIMALS

Many of us have other animals in addition to birds. If you do, allow your bird out only when you can observe all interaction carefully. If your bird is bitten by a cat or a dog, or if the cat or dog has licked or taken your bird in his mouth, take the bird to the vet immediately. The cat or dog saliva is toxic to birds, and requires an antidote without which the bird will die in about forty-eight to seventy-two hours. Each twelve-hour period that passes without treatment decreases the bird's chance of survival. Think of this bite as the reaction some humans have to bee stings.

Dog and cat saliva is toxic to birds; remember to monitor your pets' interactions.

BROKEN BONES

Fractures occur rarely, but given the Quaker parrot's active, inquisitive nature, they cannot be ruled out. If your bird breaks a leg or wing, wrap the bird gently in a towel and take him to your vet, who will know how to splint the bone. If you are told to bind the bird's wing to his body, use the gauze bandage in your first-aid kit.

HOSPITAL CAGE

If your bird requires first aid from you and follow-up care from your vet, he may also need to be kept in a hospital cage, with perches placed low to the floor and food handy. Your vet will be able to advise you if this is necessary. I keep on hand small plastic pet carriers; I use each one only for one bird or pair of birds. The sides are straight and the lid has openings to allow the free flow of air through the top of the carrier. I put small removable perches in this cage, near the bottom, with food dishes placed on the wall nearby with suction cups. I cover the floor with plain white paper towels.

The Animal Toxicology Hotline

If your bird eats something poisonous, you can call this hotline for information on what to do immediately. Have on hand the name of the substance you believe poisoned your bird. If it is a manufactured item, have the product name and the amount the bird ingested.

Although the number is on an 800 line, each call will cost you $30. In some cases, the manufacturer of the product will pay the cost, but don't count on it. Keep this number posted and in your bird's first-aid kit: **1-800-548-2423**.

Molting, Feather Plucking and Other Feather Problems

If you find feathers around the house or in the bottom of the cage, how can you tell if your bird is sick, or if the loss is due to the natural process of molting?

Just as animals lose and replace skin, birds lose and replace feathers. With some birds that are kept in warm homes, this can be a constant process. With others, it will occur once or twice a year. Factors determining how often the molt will occur can include weather, humidity and number of daylight hours, as well as general nutrition and health.

A bird who is molting may lose what seems to be an alarming number of feathers. Suddenly you will find them everywhere, big and little, down feathers, as well as tail and

---

A FIRST-AID KIT

It's easy to put together a kit that will help you take care of your bird if he injures himself. Keep these supplies in a separate box in a handy place.

A clean towel and paper towels

Sterile gauze pads

Sterile gauze pads and bandage roll

Masking tape or non-allergenic surgical tape

Petroleum jelly

Cornstarch, flour or styptic powder (must be powder)

A notepad and pen to write down vet's instructions

A small flashlight (pen light)

Blunt-edged tweezers

Needle-nosed pliers

Magnifying glass

Sterile water

Pedialyte, unflavored

Chlorhexidine (never use hydrogen peroxide on a bird)

Wire cutters

Pure aloe vera

Number of your veterinarian and the Animal Poison Hotline

wing feathers. The amazing thing is that you will not see bald patches on your bird while he molts. Shortly after you begin to see the lost feathers, you will notice small pin feathers growing on your bird, most noticeably on his head.

Your Quaker will do a lot of preening when he is molting.

He can preen himself and remove the feather casings from feathers on the rest of his body, but he cannot reach those on his head. If he will allow you to, you can gently remove each casing with your fingernails after the blood has receded. If your bird will not allow you to do it, you can cuddle him in a towel after a bath and gently rub his head to remove some casings. In any case, the bird will rub his head on perches, furniture and cage sides and bars to remove the casings.

Some bald patches on a bird are easily associated with an activity. One of my birds is trying to make a nest box of a wooden bread box. As she forces her head into the inner corners, she rubs off the tiny feathers around her beak. Because I know how she loses these feathers, the patches are of no concern. If I didn't know this, I would take her to her vet for a check-up.

Feather picking is behavior in which a bird pulls, or plucks, his own feathers or sometimes a mate's feathers. If the bird is engaged in self-mutilation, the cause should be found. Feather picking can result from parasites, from low humidity in a heated or air-conditioned house or the climate in which you live, from poor nutrition or from psychological problems. Once a bird gets in the habit of picking his feathers, it may be difficult to get him to stop. If the problem is caused by low humidity, daily baths or a cold room humidifier might help. If the cause is poor nutrition, only a better diet will remedy the situation.

If your bird begins to pick his feathers, take him to your vet to rule out all physical causes. If neither disease nor parasites are the culprit, it's time to analyze the problem more carefully. First, look at what might have changed around the time the bird began picking his feathers. Did you move the cage, add a pet, have guests, hang a new picture on the wall or change his food or the plants near his cage? Are you feeding the bird less often or at different times than you used to feed him? If you can, remove the cause of stress.

If you have ruled out stress as the cause, consider simple boredom. Quaker parrots are active, curious, intelligent birds. They need something to keep their minds occupied or they will turn to pulling feathers to pass the time. Lots of toys (rotated often) and plenty of time to play outside of the cage with sufficient attention from you should prevent this from starting.

When to See an Avian Veterinarian

You should take your bird for his first veterinary visit shortly after you buy him—preferably on your way home. This means you will have researched and located the best vet prior to buying the bird.

Thereafter, to keep your vet familiar with you and your bird, you should take the bird in once a year for a well-bird check-up. This check-up should also uncover subtle problems that were not obvious to you. Ask the vet to do a thorough blood screen and fecal culture.

Otherwise, you should call your avian vet at the first sign of illness, or in the case of injury, such as broken bones or serious burns. Make an appointment and take the bird in for an exam.

Remember, an avian vet is one who has been specially trained to work with birds and has passed a qualifying exam. A vet who sees mostly cats and dogs will not be able to treat a sick bird or determine if a bird has health problems.

Enjoying
Your

part three

Quaker Parrot

Having **Fun**
with Your
Quaker Parrot

Have you ever watched a bird show and wondered how the trainer taught the bird those tricks? Successful trainers watch their birds carefully to learn about their natural behaviors. They then plan tricks that are based on these actions. You can do this too.

Teaching Tricks

If your bird enjoys calling out, you can teach her to answer when you call her name. This training must be done in increments. Call the bird's name. If she makes a noise—any noise—praise her and give her a treat. After she has made this step, call again and reward only a larger step, like a louder noise, until you get to the call stage you are looking for.

If your bird loves to spread her wings as she stretches, you can easily turn this into a trick. Each time she stretches, you can say a cue word, such as "Eagle!" The goal will be to teach your bird to spread her wings whenever you say "Eagle!"

Quaker parrots are bright, active birds with well-developed senses of humor. Taking part in tricks will be an enjoyable outlet for some of her natural energy, a wonderful way for you and your feathered clown to interact. Use whatever props you want. At pet stores, bird shows and in the advertisements in bird-related magazines you will find accessories for these activities, such as bowling alleys, bicycles, basketball hoops and balls—most of which will come with instruction books. Quaker parrots are perfect for this kind of activity, and you will find it thoroughly entertaining.

POTTY TRAINING?

The best trick of all? Potty training. Some Quakers will train themselves, but you may not want to wait until your bird decides this would be a good idea. Potty training is easy to do. Begin by watching your bird to see how often she eliminates waste. If this is your first bird, you may be surprised at how often this happens—every fifteen to twenty minutes! I usually put a bird in her cage to observe the time intervals. Each time the bird goes potty, say "Go potty!" This helps her associate the action with the phrase.

The next step is to take your bird out of her cage just before you expect her to eliminate next. Put your Quaker on the spot you want to use for that purpose, such as the cage door, a cage-top perch or a T-stand. Say, "Go potty!" Understand that this may not happen the first time you try it, nor may it happen for several sessions, but if you continue to use the phrase when your bird defecates, she will make the connection. When she does, offer high praise, perhaps a treat, but most certainly a hug, a kiss on the top of her head and a "Good bird!" said with enthusiasm.

Thereafter, if your bird begins to get restless, quickly transport her to the acceptable place and request that she go potty. To help reinforce your bird's training, keep track of the time while your Quaker is out of her cage. At fifteen-minute intervals, be sure to return the bird to her cage to potty. If you fail to do this, you are doing a great disservice to your bird by sending mixed messages. She cannot fly, so she will depend on you for transportation to help keep up the training.

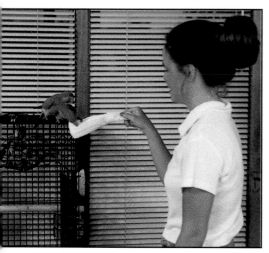

Quakers love to play games and interact with their owners.

JUST HAVING FUN

Now that you are all set up and have gotten acquainted with your Quaker parrot, it's time to do what you intended all along: Have fun! There is hardly any better companion to have fun with than a well-trained Quaker parrot.

Two reasons Quakers are so much fun are their boundless enthusiasm for life and the energy level that backs it up. These birds are, in many ways, like small children. They play hard, and they attack everything they do with great enthusiasm.

ABOUT PLAY GYMS

If you have a play gym for your bird, you can introduce new toys there, as well as in the cage. This is also a good place to begin teaching tricks. Don't leave your Quaker on her play gym for long periods of time: She may become territorial and difficult to approach. Because your bird's wings are clipped, be sure to offer a ladder to various places she is allowed to go. A swing hanging over the play gym would also be a good idea. My husband and I started with a T-stand for our most active bird. Soon it was obvious that this was not enough, so we built a swing set above the T-stand using welded chain, plastic rings and ladders. He loved it and used up a lot of energy. We taught him to swing upside down with his wings spread. He soon learned that this was an acceptable place to scream and run around like crazy.

TRICKS WITH TOYS!

Bells are another great Quaker favorite, and you will be delighted to see your bird learn to ring a bell. Choose medium-size bells made for cockatiel-size birds. Avoid the round "jingle bell" types; the slits in their sides make them dangerous to beaks that might easily become trapped there.

After your bird gets used to her toys, and you have watched her play for awhile, you can begin to see which behaviors she particularly enjoys and repeats. Using these, you can teach your Quaker parrot tricks that you will both enjoy.

If your bird likes to climb ladders, for instance, you can begin by rewarding her with a tiny bit of a favorite treat each time she climbs a ladder. Add a word to the trick, such as "Up!" Say the word each time the bird successfully climbs the ladder; then give her the treat. After a time, you can only give the treat when the bird goes up the ladder after you have said the word. When she has learned this, you can add other elements, such as ringing a bell or flying to a swing.

The play gym is a good place to introduce new toys to your Quaker.

TALKING

If your bird learns to talk, you may want to tie certain tricks into talking. This might include a word from you that will elicit a certain response, such as "Eagle!" to which your bird responds "Cock-a-doodle-doo." This trick would require a bird with a talent for talking. Teach the bird to say "Cock-a-doodle-doo," first. Then, every time he says this phrase, reward him with a treat.

After he has come to expect a treat, you can begin by saying "Eagle!" Ask another person to "model" by responding with the chicken phrase. Give the friend a treat each time, in front of your watching pet. The next step is to say "Eagle!" to your pet and then reward any sound she makes. After a while, you should only reward sounds that begin to resemble the phrase. Model it with your friend often. Eventually, your bird will respond with the correct phrase.

Once your bird learns how to spread her wings when you say "Eagle!" you can tie in talking skills as well.

LEARNING TRICKS STEP-BY-STEP

One of my birds learned to say "Night night." Because we thought that was such fun, I wanted to teach him to say "Night night" when I held him on his back in the palm of my hand. This behavior requires a lot of trust. I waited to begin until I was sure I had his absolute trust. Of course, I also waited until I trusted him; I was sure he would not bite me even if he was a bit afraid. I began by holding him in my hand; not on my fingers, not standing on his feet, but cupped in my hand. This took months. Each time he got a little closer to my goal, I rewarded him with a tiny piece of cheddar cheese—a huge favorite that I did not give him at any other time. The next step was to get him to accept being turned on his side, using my right hand to turn him in my left hand. This took months. I only rewarded him for each incremental move toward my goal. If he did not want to practice, I backed off, but he did not get the cheese.

In about a year, he would let me hold him on his back. Then I began to say "Night night," as soon as he was on his back. Again, at first, if he made a noise at all, I rewarded him. If he made no noise, he earned no cheese. Step by step he advanced, until about three months later, I could flip him on his back and he would say, "Night night." This is not a monumental trick; however, it does illustrate that it is up to you to set an attainable goal and to maintain a calm, rewarding atmosphere for training. It is also up to you to understand that it may take months for the bird to learn the trick—the more complicated the trick, the longer you should plan to take. The more natural the action, the easier the trick will be to teach.

Holding your Quaker on her back takes a lot of time and trust.

Each Quaker Is Unique

Each bird is an individual with her own personality. You will soon know what she will do and what she won't. Some birds will be too active to want to take part in anything as passive as cuddling while you watch television. Those are the ones that will love learning to climb a ladder and ring a bell, or fly from swing to swing on cue. Other tricks you might try include climbing down a ladder or a rope on cue, putting things in a cup or toy and asking for a treat, either with a sound or a word. How about "Please?" Practicing while teaching the trick and showing off the results will give both you and your bird hours of fun.

You can teach your Quaker parrot to say "Please?" when asking for a treat.

115

chapter 10

Answers
for
New Owners

Since I began this book, I have searched for people who have recently bought Quakers to learn those questions that concern them most. I've included the most asked questions here, hoping to answer some of your questions, too. Each of these pet owners had owned his or her bird from a few days to a few months when I recorded our conversations.

Q: I brought my bird home about two days ago, and she shakes whenever I come near. Is she cold or afraid of me? What can I do?

A: Although I suspect that your bird is still unaccustomed to you and the rest of her new surroundings, we need to look at the whole picture. Is the temperature inside your house about the same as that of the pet store or the breeding facility? If there is a ceiling vent in the room, tape the ends of slender strips of paper to it. Watch the strips when the heating or air-conditioning system is on. They will show you which direction the air blows. If your bird is in a direct pathway, move the cage. Also make sure she is not in front of a window or doorway.

If temperature is not the problem, then make sure your bird feels secure. Remember that she is in a new environment. Try to put yourself in her place. Back the cage against an interior wall, preferably in a corner to give her security on two sides. She will soon learn that no one can suddenly appear and startle her from either of those sides.

Beyond that, simply take your time approaching and gaining the trust of your new little pet. Talk to her softly and reassuringly. Use her name often. Offer treats. In a few months, you will won-der what happened to that shy bird you once knew.

Q: My bird and I just had our first training session, and I no-ticed that his feet are hot. Does this mean that he has a fever? How do I know if he has a fever?

A: A bird has a higher metab-olism and heart rate than a human, and his normal tem-perature is higher as well. Some signs of illness include decreased appetite, diarrhea, discolored droppings, inac-tivity, sleeping on two feet, fluffed feathers and sit-ting on the bottom of the cage. Those signs will tell you to talk to your avian veterinarian, who will know how to take and evaluate your bird's temperature.

Why are my bird's feet hot?

Q: I know my bird needs clean water to drink, but she keeps getting in her water dish to bathe. How can I keep her out of it?

117

A: Most Quaker parrots enjoy bathing, and they will decide when and where they will do so. Consider using a water bottle for drinking and a dish outside of the cage for bathing. Remember, though, that this bottle must be exchanged with a clean one once a day. Keep two or three on hand, and wash them in the dishwasher to remove all bacteria.

Q: My bird's feathers get dark, almost black, when she gets wet. Is this normal?

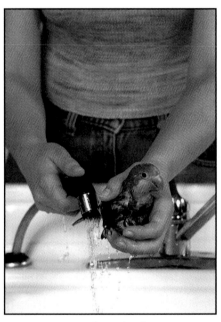

Why do my Quaker parrot's feathers look dark when they are wet?

A: When you look at your Quaker parrot, the colors you see are the result of the way in which light is reflected off of the dry feathers. After your bird has taken a bath, her wet feathers will reflect light differently than when dry, making them look dark.

Q: How many toys are too many? I go to buy one or two toys and find myself walking out with many more. My bird's cage is looking kind of crowded.

A: You probably cannot buy too many toys for a Quaker parrot, but don't put all of them in the cage at one time. Instead, put a few in the cage, and then rotate them with others every few days. Do this when the bird is out of the cage—and out of sight. He might not want your hands in the cage.

Q: My bird bit me. Does that mean that she doesn't like me anymore?

A: Birds bite for all kinds of reasons. If you and your bird had a good relationship previously, more than likely she was simply expressing one of many emotions, including surprise, anger, fear, jealousy or possessiveness. She might also have been hungry, over-tired or out of sorts.

On the other hand, your bird could be feeling unwell. Watch her closely to see if she shows any other signs of illness. One other possibility is that your bird is trying to control you. If, after eliminating all other possibilities, you decide that this is the case, you can train her again, making sure she knows who is in charge.

Q: My Quaker's tail feathers break. What causes this and what can I do to prevent it?

A: First, take your bird to your avian veterinarian for a check-up. Next, look at the cage. Is it large enough, or do the bird's tail feathers drag against the bars? Do the perches need to be moved to accommodate his tail?

If nothing is physically wrong and your bird is young, he may not have adjusted to having his wings clipped. If he tries to fly and flutters to the floor, a young bird may break his fall with his tail, damaging the feathers. In time, if you train him to stay on his perch until you take him from place to place, the tail will grow in. This requires that you follow through, though. If you leave him long enough to become bored, or without toys to play with, he will try to fly.

What could be making my Quaker parrot stressed out?

Q: What foods or drinks are dangerous for my bird?

A: The list is short, actually: Avocado, rhubarb leaves and chocolate can kill a bird. All have chemicals toxic to birds. Also avoid excessive sugar and salt, as well as overly fatty foods. Your bird should never drink alcohol. Finally, avoid any large seed pits, as well as apple seeds. All of these store toxins that can kill your bird.

Q: Does my bird need a bath? My Quaker parrot is six months old and loves water. He likes to dive in his bathing dish. Is this safe? How often should I let him bathe?

A: All birds need to bathe to keep their feathers clean and in good shape, but Quaker parrots really enjoy it. Daily bathing also helps prevent Quakers from beginning that destructive process called feather plucking. Some Quakers do like to dive in their bath, and why not? Sounds like fun to me, especially on a warm day.

How often should my Quaker parrot bathe?

Is my Quaker parrot a "closet talker?"

Q: My Quaker talks only when we are out of the room. Why does he do this, and how can we get him to talk in front of us?

A: This is often referred to as "closet talking." Usually, the bird begins to talk in front of people when he's comfortable. One of my birds does this. She practices in private and then, when she is ready, she will talk when we are in the same room. Usually by that time, she has perfected the word or phrase.

Q: I am afraid to clip my bird's nails. I know they are too long because they curl and she cannot stand comfortably. What should I do?

A: Take your bird to your avian vet right away before she snags a nail and loses blood unnecessarily. Possibly, the vet will clip the nails a little bit on the first visit and then will ask you to return every few days for more gradual clipping until the nails are the correct length. On the other hand, the vet may clip the bird's nails back to a shorter length, using styptic powder to stop the bleeding. Your bird's feet will be sore for several days, though. Do not let her toenails overgrow again. Ask your vet to teach you how to clip the nails and keep up with the chore.

Q: When Quaker parrots talk, do they just mimic human speech sounds, or do they understand what they say?

A: Quaker parrots are intelligent animals. My best guess is that they understand what they are saying—to a degree. They know when you said the phrase they have picked up, and can attach the words to whatever was happening when you said them. You will find that they talk appropriately—in the most surprising ways. Be careful what you say around your bird, especially if you say it with a lot of emotion!

part four

Beyond
the
Basics

chapter 11

References

Books

Athan, Mattie Sue. *Guide to the Quaker Parrot.* New York: Barron's, 1997.

Athan, Mattie Sue. *Guide to a Well-Behaved Parrot.* New York: Barron's, 1993.

Athan, Mattie Sue. *Keeping Quaker Parrots Tame.* Companion Animal Education Foundation, 1997.

Barber, T.X. *The Human Nature of Birds.* New York: St. Martin's Press, 1993.

Bedford, Duke of. *Parrots and Parrot-like Birds.* New Jersey: TFH Publications, 1969.

Doane, Bonnie Munro and Thomas Qualkinbush. *My Parrot, My Friend: An Owner's Guide to Parrot Behavior.* New York: Howell Book House, 1994.

Feduccia, Alan. *The Age of Birds.* New Jersey: Harvard University Press, 1980.

Forshaw, Joseph M. Illustrated by William T. Cooper. *Parrots of the World.* New Jersey: TFH Publications, 1978.

Gallerstein, Gary A. *The Complete Bird Owner's Handbook*. New York: Howell Book House, 1994.

Greeson, Linda. *The Charming Little Quaker*. Greeson's Baby Parrots, 1995.

Humphries, Joanne L. *The Quaker Booklet: The Little Green Tyrant*. The Bird House, 1992.

Jordan, Theresa and Alan. *The Quaker Parakeet Handbook*. Jordan Enterprises, 1997.

Low, Rosemary. *Parrots: Their Care and Breeding*. London: Blandford Press, 1992.

Lowell, Michele. *Your Pet Bird, A Buyer's Guide*. New York: Henry Holt and Company, 1994.

Murphy, Dr. Joel. *How to Care for Your Pet Bird*. Clearwater, Fla.: MABH Publishing, 1994.

Parker, Dennis. *Parrots as a Hobby*. New Jersey: TFH Publications, 1994.

Stunkard, DVM. *A Guide to Diagnosis, Treatment and Husbandry of Caged Birds*. Veterinary Medicine Publishing Company, 1982.

Weiner, Jonathan. *The Beak of the Finch*. New York: Alfred A. Knopf, 1994.

Magazines

Bird Talk. Monthly magazine devoted to pet bird ownership. Back issues or back articles on Quakers available on request. Subscription information: P.O. Box 57347, Boulder, CO 80322-7347

Birds USA. Annual magazine aimed at first-time bird owners. Look for it in your local pet store or bookstore.

Caged Bird Hobbyist. This magazine for pet bird owners is published seven times a year. Subscription information: 5400 NW 84 Ave., Miami, FL 33166-3333

Natural Pet. Monthly magazine devoted to the best in natural care for all pets. Available at your local pet or bookstore.

Newsletter

The Quaker News. Edited by Linda Greeson. Subscription information: The Quaker News, P.O. Box 609, Fruitland Park, FL 34731-0609

On-Line Resources

Quaker-specific sites abound on the Internet. These run the gamut from sites run by breeders to bulletin boards where new owners can post questions, which will be answered by other Quaker owners, breeders and animal behaviorists. You will have to sift through this information for accuracy.

If you belong to an on-line service, look for its pet site (sometimes included in more general topics, such as "Hobbies and Interests" or, more specifically, "Pets"). If you have Internet access, use your Web browser or WebCrawler to search for "parrots," "pet birds," "Quaker Parrots" or "Monk Parrots."

The URLs listed were valid as of publication. We can take no responsibility for the accuracy of information posted on any site.

Birds n Ways, Winged Wisdom. An on-line magazine with information on bird care, including such topics as first aid, toxins and nutrition.
http://www.208.5.192.104/wisdom/ww2e.htm

The Quaker Parakeet website. Run by Theresa and Alan Jordan. This site is full of information, from an on-line newsletter to basic information on nutrition, toys, photos, a mail bag and links to many other Quaker-related sites.
http://www.smalltalk.bitshop.com

Research on feral Quakers can be found at these three sites. For other sites, set your web browser to look for "Quaker Parrots" and "feral" or "Monk Parrots" and "feral."
http://www.utexas.edu/depts/grg/ustudent/gcraft/
   fall96/huebner/projects/gif/monkmap.gif
http://www.master.net/aviary/gpage/
http://nasw.org/users/kcarr

The Online Book of Parrots. This is an excellent listing of many parrots, including Quakers, found under the scientific name *Myiopsitta*.
http://www.ub.tu-clausthal.de/PAhtml/aratingidae/
    myiopsitta.html

There is an on-line posting of an article on Quaker Parakeets, "Parrots and Plunder," from the July 1997 issue of *Scientific American*.
http://www.sciam.com/0797issue/scidit2.html

Webmaster Jon-Mark Davey runs this well-organized site, which is full of information and web connections.
http://flinet.com/~jmdavey/quakerville.htm

Bird Clubs

The American Federation of Aviculture
P.O. Box 56218
Phoenix, AZ 85079-6128

Avicultural Society of America
P.O. Box 5516
Riverside, CA 92517-5517

International Avicultural Society
P.O. Box 280383
Memphis, TN 38168

Society of Parrot Breeders and Exhibitors
P.O. Box 369
Groton, MA 01450